FROM **BRITAIN** TO **BUNNY**

*A Playmate's Journey Living
the American Dream*

BY
ZOË GREGORY

Ballast Books, LLC
www.ballastbooks.com

ISBN: 978-1-962202-25-1

Printed in the United States of America

Published by Ballast Books
www.ballastbooks.com

For more information, bulk orders, appearances, or speaking requests, please email: info@ballastbooks.com

TABLE OF CONTENTS

INTRODUCTION

Never in my wildest dreams did I think I would go from being a single mother on welfare to living my best life in the Playboy Mansion with one of the biggest superstars in the world.

My story starts like so many others. I was a rebellious teenager, profiting from the rave scene, taking risks, and not suffering the consequences. When I set out to prove my love to my boyfriend, I finally had to face the music—but was also given the greatest gift of my life, in my beautiful son. This moment forced me to grow up. I began to take every opportunity I could to get through the trials and tribulations of single motherhood.

I had a dream, and I was determined. Having grown up in England, I wanted more than anything to emigrate to the US. I wanted something bigger, and Hollywood was the place to go. I wanted to get away from the life I was living before it was too late and to give my son a better life with better opportunities. While fate and luck played a big part in my journey, I am living proof that manifestation works—as long as you are willing to put in some work, too.

Even when I hit rock bottom and lost everything, I never gave up. I remained strategic and focused on my goals, and in the end, everything worked out in my favour. But it was Hugh Hefner who escalated my dreams—without Hef, I never would have dreamed big enough to get where I am today. Thanks to his influence, I have fulfilled more of my ambitions and goals, from competing in and winning fitness competitions to flight attending on private charter jets around the world to now writing my life story.

He handed me my freedom and set me up for the rest of my life.

Hugh Hefner and Playboy gave me something different from what other girls may have achieved through the company. It was more than being featured in a magazine; it was a path to a whole new life and future. The gratitude I have for being involved with the legendary company that will forever hold a legacy is immeasurable. I'm still living my dreams, but I will never forget where I came from.

I wanted to share my story with the many women who have a dream like mine or have experienced similar situations in life. No matter the cards you are dealt, what counts is how you choose to play them.

You can take the girl out of the tough streets of London, but you can't take the tough streets of London out of the girl, and I tell it like it is. This is my story, with no bullshit.

CHAPTER 1

CHILDHOOD

As a youngster, I was fond of people-watching.

I kept to myself most of the time. I observed and interpreted the conversations between my parents. I observed how people's emotions changed based on the words of others.

Born and raised in London's Camden Town in the late 1970s, I was a pretty typical kid growing up. I did gymnastics on the weekends and enjoyed playing sports, getting quite competitive during events at school. You could say I was more of a tomboy, doing boys' things. I enjoyed the challenge.

My parents were super cool, a very down-to-earth couple; they often smoked weed freely in the house. They were popular and had many friends, and I was always allowed around the adults in the house. I listened to their conversations and benefited from their great taste in music, which they always had playing. My father owned a great sound system and a large selection of vinyl records that he had collected over the years.

My mother was into fashion. She always had the nicest clothes and always had her hair and makeup done; she was a beautiful, well-groomed woman. She also competed in beauty pageants when she was younger. Since she had a great eye for fashion, as a side business, she would buy and sell clothes to her friends. She was an artist with an expert hand for drawing and beautiful penmanship. I was born on her birthday.

My father was a skilled handyman who worked on restoring exotic cars. He could fix anything and seemingly knew everything about every trade. He always had a solution to any problem. I really loved that about him. He was heroic to me. He was a genuine guy with a lot of different friends from diverse cultures. He was a bodybuilder during my childhood; he was very fit and had tattoos.

We always had nice things, including many exotic animals. We had fish tanks, snakes, and a couple dogs. I loved my father's compassion for animals. My father was very fortunate, but sometimes he trusted the wrong people. We were raided a couple of times by the police. My parents would always tell me the police had made a mistake and raided the wrong house, but I knew more than they thought. I was a very observant kid.

My father had a temper and would often have aggressive moments, breaking things and shouting. I stayed out of his way when he got angry—he would take it out on anyone who got in his way. One time, I took all his records out of their covers, placed them on the floor, and proceeded to skate on them with my feet sliding from side to side. I paid the consequences for that. He had a heavy hand when I was naughty. He never hit me otherwise, but I sure did ask for it when I did get smacked. He didn't take anyone's shit.

I never wanted to be apart from my best friend, Nicky, who lived across the road from me. We did everything together. We always talked about our dreams of moving to Hollywood. We looked very much alike—everyone thought we were sisters, both blonde and pretty. I had a lot of friends who lived on the same street, and we remain friends to this day.

My mum made me pretty clothes on her sewing machine, so I would have dresses and skirts with frills that no other girls had. She would plait my hair to make it wavy and put bows on each side. She took a lot of pride in her family. We were always well presented and put together.

My mum submitted photos of me to a kids' modelling agency. They were very interested in representing me. I was seven years old and enjoying school at the time.

During my years at primary school, my mum or a family member frequently picked me up during school hours to take me to auditions and castings that were sent from my modelling agency. It began to interfere with my schooling, and I was getting upset about missing my friends at school. I had been working a lot; I didn't understand why everyone fussed over me being a child model. I had been regularly shooting catalogues for *Mothercare*, a clothing and product catalogue for mothers and children. Later, I shot a Horizon Holidays TV commercial. When I returned to school, all the kids talked about how they had seen me on the TV.

I asked my mother where the money was for all the work I had been doing, and we started butting heads about it. I protested and didn't want to go on auditions anymore. I remember feeling resentful. My mother told me she used the money I'd earned to buy my clothes and school items, but I never believed her.

During my last years of primary school, I was rather destructive. My parents were arguing a lot as they would often be in bad moods. I had a new baby brother at home—Louie. I was seven when he was born, and we were not that close growing up. I think what was going on in the home made me act up in school. I felt left out and ignored, and I would act up a lot because of that.

My mother's side of the family is Greek, and they were very much like the movie *My Big Fat Greek Wedding*: loud, obnoxious, always cooking and forcing you to eat. My maternal grandmother, Dora, was a lovely, sweet, caring lady who was very protective of me. She taught me how to speak Greek fluently when I was nine years old. She was very wise. My aunty and uncle dabbled in the fashion industry too.

My father's side was English and French. I didn't see much of them growing up.

Secondary school was fun until homework became a challenge. That's when I rebelled. I was always out of the house, always wanting to be with my friends, always absent from school. I had become quite popular from being in the modelling industry . . . I was overly friendly, and I had a lot of charisma. People would mistake that for being flirtatious. I got in many physical fights with other girls because they were jealous of me.

A group of friends and I hung around in Queen's Crescent, and we experimented with a lot of different drugs. It was 1989 and I was fourteen, smoking cigarettes and weed, taking XTC and acid, and inhaling huffing gas. We were a tight group of friends and all still very young, but hardly any of them went to school. Most of the boys would go earning (thieving), whether it was stealing car stereos or anything else they could get their hands on. My dad's car was broken into a few times; I'm sure the culprit was one of my friends, but that was the way things were. We would order pizzas from a phone box and have them delivered to an address in Queen's Crescent, just so we could steal the pizza delivery motorbike. We spent many cold days and nights hanging around not doing much, but we were always together; I never wanted to be home.

My mother gave me hell. She was an excellent judge of character and read me like a book; I think she knew me better than I knew myself at times. I was becoming out of control and wouldn't listen to my parents at all.

When I was fifteen years old, my mum would get angry with me for staying over at my boyfriend's house. I'm sure she knew we were having sex. My boyfriend and I were very much alike. We always had fun earning together. We were together for a while, on and off.

One day when I returned home from spending the night at his house, my mother's instincts kicked in, and she accused me of being pregnant. She took me to the doctor for a pregnancy test. She was right: I was pregnant—three and half months. There wasn't even a thought of whether I should keep it. My mother had already decided I was going to have an abortion; the situation devastated her. I think I was too young to get affected emotionally at the time, but it did affect me later in life and still does to this day. After I had the abortion, things changed between my boyfriend and me; we broke up even though we still had feelings for each other.

My mother finally told me if I was not going to continue with school, I needed to go and find a job, start paying rent, and help her out.

CHAPTER 2

REBELLION AND A BABY

I found a job as a junior at a local hairdresser's shop a few minutes from where I lived. I quite enjoyed it; this is where I really got into beauty and taking more time and effort on my appearance. Learning about hair styling, I was soon colouring hair for my friends and family. It was the first time I had experienced having money in my pocket legitimately, money I had earned myself by working for it. I was feeling quite independent, which gave me a sense of maturity.

My best friend Nicky and I had been curious about going out to the clubs. We were now fifteen years old and so eager to go and have some fun.

We went to Kensington High Street to see a club one of our friends had told us about. We didn't think we would get in, but we gave it a try; we had dolled ourselves up, looking older than we were. As it turned out, we had no trouble getting in. The club, Dejavous, was the place to be. We started going regularly. We also would go to another club in Camden Town called the Camden Palace. They held a rave every weekend put on by "Orange." Nicky ended up getting close with the MC who performed there, so we were always on the guest list and able to go in the DJ box.

I ended up having the best times of my life at the Camden Palace with my friends, the drugs, the dancing, the music, the laser lights. Everyone knew everyone, and the music was always good since Orange booked the best DJs. The best thing about the new rave scene was it united everyone from all the areas of Camden. Until that scene arose, the different boroughs hadn't gotten along. It was a "streets" rule to stay in the borough you came from.

By 1988, the rave scene was booming, and my friends and I would attend all of the raves at the Camden Palace, Orange at the Rocket, Sunrise, Biology, Telepathy, and many other venues. When we weren't going out at the weekends, all we really had to do was smoke, drink, do drugs, steal motorbikes and joy ride, and go earning. We would go over to Hampstead Heath and watch the sun come up and go on crazy adventures whilst under the influence.

I had figured out that there was a profit to be made from selling XTC tablets at raves. I started to make fake XTC. I would buy zinc vitamin tablets, as they most closely resembled the real XTC tablet; then I would use a knife to carve a dove-shaped bird so they looked like Dove XTC tabs. I would coat them with nail-bite solution so it would give the bitter taste like real XTC. I was selling fake tabs for £20 each and selling five hundred or more a night. I never got caught, and I never had any comebacks fortunately.

Around this time, I started going out with Brad. He was in my circle of friends from my neighbourhood. He was a little older than me, and we would always walk home together from the Crescent hangout or from the Camden Palace. Brad was a hustler, a good earner, a pretty good criminal. He went out every day earning (stealing), so he always had something good to sell: car stereos, mountain bikes, cameras, mobile phones, jewellery, office equipment, you name it. He got caught one too many times and ended up in jail—always in the local prison—but I stuck by him. It was 1991. We were heavily involved by this time, and he was practically living with me at my parents' house. I wrote to him and visited him regularly in prison. He had done nearly a year in jail when they released him.

My mother and father wanted to move to Cyprus for a while and wanted me and my younger brother to go too. My brother was still very young. I really didn't want to go with them. I was too involved with my friends and Brad, and I wanted to stay in London. So I told my parents that I was not going and would stay and live at the house with Brad. They were not happy about leaving me behind.

They packed up and left for Cyprus while I was waiting for Brad to return from jail. He was finally released. We had really missed each other, and the year he was gone had flown by. He asked me to prove my love for him by having his baby. I felt secure with him that he would always be able to provide for us because he always had money from earning. I knew I would have to live with the risk of him getting caught again, always being on edge, not knowing if he'd come home in the evening or I would get a call from the nick (police station). I threw my contraceptive pills out of the window in front of him to prove I was willing to get pregnant and have his baby. Whilst trying for a baby, we continued to go to the raves, sell duds (fake XTC), and have a good time, though I stopped taking all drugs and stopped smoking and drinking once I came off the pill.

We were still making good money together and continued to. When I was around seven months pregnant, I was starting to feel a lot more tired and would stay home while he hustled. I saved up and purchased a car, and we applied for a council flat with Camden Council whilst still living at my parents'.

I had a great pregnancy; I never experienced morning sickness. I was just hungry all the time. I started working out while I was pregnant since I was gaining a lot of weight. I still hadn't really finished developing my breasts. I think I was a late bloomer. I hated being so flat chested. Even though I had not fully developed my breasts yet, they hurt during the pregnancy and were so sensitive I couldn't even touch them. I was hoping not to get any stretch marks over my body.

We had the best of everything for our child. I loved shopping for my baby.

I dreaded telling my parents that I was pregnant. I think my mother had an idea this would happen while they were away in Cyprus. She always had a sixth sense, but at least they were so far away that they couldn't really do much. I finally gave them the news, and they were not happy with me. I know my mum wanted to be close to me while I was going through my pregnancy. At least my grandmother was always there for me, making sure the house was stocked up with food.

My mum returned to London to visit me and stayed by my side during the last month of pregnancy. She wanted to be at the birth to make sure everything went well. My contractions started in the late evening of 23 July 1992, and I gave birth at 12:45 a.m. on 24 July 1992. I was so grateful my mother was by my side. I had a natural birth, only receiving gas to help with the pain, and oh boy did I regret not having the epidural. Lewis was born seven pounds, twelve ounces; Brad was nowhere to be found. I was devastated he couldn't be there for the birth. I later found out that he was at the Camden Palace, enjoying himself. His mobile phone didn't work in the underground venue. I was so hurt, but soon I was too distracted with my beautiful baby boy to stay bothered about it.

Lewis came into my world. What a beautiful little thing he was. I think I really needed this in my life. It gave me a sense of direction, responsibility, and motivation. Thinking about our future, I was in awe. I couldn't stop looking at him.

Lewis's father wasn't really present. He was always out earning. Meanwhile, I was learning how to be a mother. I was really enjoying motherhood, and I wanted to move out of my parents' home to have my own space and independence. After eight months had passed, we received an offer for a flat, and Brad, Lewis, and I moved out of my parents' house. That's when my mum and dad came back to the UK permanently. I think it was because of my situation. I felt guilty about that.

I took the two-bedroom flat we were offered, and we quickly moved in. Even though we were doing well, I had applied for a grant to decorate and furnish the place. We had a nice budget and were not hurting for money at the time. I was so proud of my first home; it was on the top floor with a great view in the heart of Camden Town. It was the first time I'd felt house-proud; I felt so grown even though I'd just turned eighteen. I felt like an adult. It's amazing how motherhood can grow you up so quickly.

CHAPTER 3

REACHING ADULTHOOD AND TURNING THINGS AROUND

It was 1995, and Lewis was having his third birthday. His father and I hadn't been spending much time together anymore. I think I had gone through postnatal depression without knowing I had it. I also felt like I had evolved without him and become a different person who had found new morals, new standards, new needs and desires. In time, I couldn't stand the father of my son; we had drifted apart. I didn't want him to touch me. I was trying to keep the peace in our home, but I was so miserable. I remember feeling sick that I had to have intercourse or any intimacy with him. I remember calculating how and when I could leave him and be able to fend for myself and my son. I made an agreement with myself that once Lewis turned four years old and could go to nursery, I would have my independence and some time back, and maybe I could get back to work.

Around this time, things began to get aggressive in our home. Brad and I would argue a lot. I was constantly unhappy and didn't want to communicate with him. He turned violent towards me. He had a drinking problem that had gotten worse.

We had a really bad fight one day, and I just couldn't take any more. He had picked up all of our furniture and thrown it over the balcony; every single piece was down below on the grass, broken. The house was empty. I called the police when he was taking a bath. I had grabbed a large screwdriver in my hand for protection in case he came at me again. He was still in a rage, still shouting; I was crying, frantically waiting for the police to get there. I was scared for the first time in our relationship and scared for my son.

When he walked out of the bathroom, I was standing against the wall, pointing the screwdriver at him, screaming, "Don't come near me. Just get out!"

He came towards me and tried to grab it from me, but I swung the screwdriver towards him, slicing his ribs. He was naked and wet and now bleeding, shouting at me. Lewis was crying in his room.

I could hear the police radio coming from the open window in the kitchen, and I instantly felt relieved. I let the police in and explained everything. They had seen what Brad had done with all the furniture. The police told him to leave the premises and not return; they were very familiar with Brad, as he had been arrested so many times previously.

That was the big fight that ended it all between us. I had him taken off of the tenancy of the flat; it was hard for a while as I was on income support and Brad was being vindictive. I got no help from him at all.

When Lewis turned four years old and started nursery, my life became so much easier. My friends were still doing the same things, going out raving, but I felt like I was on a different path with a child.

All of a sudden, we had nothing in common. My priorities were different. I wanted to work on myself and feel happy again after being in an unhappy relationship, having depression, and suffering mentally. Going through all that physical abuse can really make you neglect yourself and not care about how you look or feel. I just felt so numb inside.

I joined the local gym and started to work out again, which really helped me mentally and physically. It was also therapeutic. The one thing that was constantly on my consciousness was how my body had changed with pregnancy; I had gained so many stretch marks on my thighs and breasts. It made me become very body conscious. How was I to be naked ever again in front of anyone? The insecurities played a big part in my mental instability. I'd always been rather fit and in good health, but I was still in a bad place mentally from my relationship with Brad.

The one friend I did have things in common with was my childhood best friend Nicky. She had a baby a year earlier than I did. We had always talked about having children together. She fell pregnant unexpectedly and didn't tell her mother until the day she was due and in labour. She was able to hide it from her family until the last minute. I always thought it was so amazing how she kept it undercover for so long. I think that her having a baby at sixteen played a big part in my decision to have a child with Brad, as it was our childhood dream from when we were kids.

Brad wasn't fond of Nicky. That's why I had not seen her much during my pregnancy or in the previous couple of years, but once I was single again, we got back in touch and carried on where we'd left off. We did everything together again. Our little boys would play together every day at the park. She mentioned we should go out on the town like we used to. I hadn't given any thought to going out, mingling, and meeting new people. I felt like my frame of mind was not ready for the new outside world. If I met someone, what about my body? How would I deal with that situation? I had gotten myself into a rut with this fear and insecurity. Was it too soon to go out and enjoy myself? Was it too soon to possibly meet someone new?

Maybe going out would be healthy for me. Meeting new people and moving on with my life was the right thing to do. My parents were happy to babysit and help me out.

I used to be such a positive, happy, and bubbly person. I wanted to get that back. I needed to be around people and socialise again. I felt like I pretty much had everything in place in my life. I had my flat and my car. I was in a good place with my independence. I had another chance at starting over again, and Lewis was an amazing, well-behaved child. I was so grateful he was too young to under-stand what was going on. What a blessing he was; he never cried, and he slept through the night. I was so fortunate.

I suppose I can't deny the fact that as I matured, I became more attractive. People would often ask if I was a model. I'd reply, "I used to be a child model, but not anymore." And in return, they would say, "Well, you should be modelling." Hearing compliments like this really gave me the confidence I needed. I find myself to be a rather modest person who does not take compliments very well, nor do I seek praise. I hadn't really had time to think about myself, about what my future held and what I wanted to do in terms of a career, especially now that I had a child. I had left school at age fourteen and didn't complete any exams, nor did I graduate. So as for being a professional with a real well-paying job, I thought I really didn't have much of a chance. But I could always get back into modelling.

One night, Nicky and I went out to the Camden Palace for a night out. She introduced me to Chris, a DJ and promoter who was friends with the guy she was seeing. He owned Orange Promotions, and every one of my friends had known of him: he put on the biggest raves every week at the Palace. I knew about him from when I used to go out. At the time, he was a big deal. He was on *Top of the Pops*, a well-known TV show, and he was a renowned music producer of the '80s and '90s. I would always hear his name on the radio advertising his events with the best DJs.

He seemed a lot more mature than me, but I found his reputation and power intriguing and a little intimidating at the same time—he had thousands of people dancing on the floor to his music. He was a master at his craft. I had never really been around someone with so much control who was doing so well for themselves. I was so very curious about this guy; he would play the music I loved and had great knowledge of the business side of running events. Then later to find out he was a music producer and had had music in the charts that he had produced . . . I was in awe. Nicky and I started going to the Camden Palace every week, and Chris and I were getting on really well. I think I was his number one fan at the time. At least that's how it felt. I found out he was fifteen years older than me and was previously a police officer. That freaked me out a bit, and he seemed very smart. I really liked being around someone who could open my eyes to new things, someone I could learn from.

I learned that he had a partnership in a business in Los Angeles, a strip club. That made me feel a little insecure. But Los Angeles? Hollywood? That is the one place I had been dreaming of going since I was a child. I confessed to him that I had always wanted to go to LA when I had the opportunity. As time went on, I really enjoyed his company. He looked at me differently; he wasn't what I had been used to. He wasn't like the people I grew up with. I started to visit him where he lived. He had a nice house that he owned. I would take the train up to see him, and my mum would babysit Lewis for me.

Chris and I were becoming intimate, but I still would not take off my top during our intimate moments. Finally I had to tell him about my son and why I had insecurities about my breasts. I was worried that having a child so young would change how guys thought about me, but I explained to him about the last couple of years and how wonderful my son was. Chris said he would eventually like to meet Lewis. I struggled a little with our intimacy, but he was attentive, showed me concern, and talked to me about my issues.

We went on to talk about breast augmentation and how it was something I was looking into, perhaps having an augmentation at some point in the near future. I was rather surprised how supportive he was—he actually offered to help me if it was something I really wanted to do.

I wanted to feel good again, and I began to get excited about how I could maybe have my breasts done—and possibly even get into modelling again. I suddenly felt like I had hope. I had faith in the future.

CHAPTER 4

MODELLING

I talked to my mother about getting my breasts done. She did not approve, and I was unsure why she was not on my side about the procedure. However, there was no stopping me. I found a surgeon in London who seemed trustworthy. Chris came with me to the consultation. At that time, the cost of breast augmentation was £2,700; Chris was willing to help me with the costs. I was twenty-one when I had my breast surgery. It was very painful, but it was worth it. As I shopped for bras and bikinis, my new size was a 34B. The procedure helped to fill out the droopy skin and helped with the stretchmarks on my breasts. I was quite happy to be naked again. I must say it improved my sex life and confidence dramatically. It changed every aspect of my life.

I had a new outlook and a new attitude. It did cross my mind that I could somehow capitalise on them. Lewis was in school now. I had a little time to myself during the day so I could visit some model agencies. I took a few Polaroids of myself and submitted them to Yvonne Paul Management and International Model Management (IMM), and both were happy to sign me to their agencies.

I could only really be considered for glamour modelling because of the type of look I had and also my height. I was a blonde, five-foot-five, busty glamour girl, and I was fine with that. I was so motivated, so hungry about this new lead in life. I cannot express how grateful I was to have Chris's positive influence around me. Just when I thought I would always hate men because of my previous experience, I had faith once again; I let my barriers down.

I had a couple of photo shoots to get pictures of my new look; I wanted to put a great portfolio together. I started casting a lot and enjoying the process of becoming a model again. My agent Yvonne called me about interest from *The Sun* tabloid newspaper to test pose for Page 3, the topless section. She advised me I should take them up on the offer. *The Sun* is the newspaper has a large circulation: 1,858,067 daily. "This is a big deal," I thought. I talked to Chris about it first. He was rather excited about it and so excited for me, but the issue was my parents. I already knew they would not approve, so I didn't even bother with telling them. I also had to consider my son and other family members. The test shoot for Page 3 did not guarantee I'd be featured. However, if I were selected, my picture would be published. I had my doubts, but I didn't want to regret not trying. Also, what other opportunities might come of it?

I went with it and shot for Page 3. I was nervous about the outcome. How would I deal with the rejection if I were not published? What would my family say if I were? How would the neighbours act towards me? I knew my father might go ballistic. This decision could really have a negative outcome . . . or it could be the best career move I'd ever made. After two weeks passed and I'd heard nothing, I pretty much felt like it wasn't going to happen. My agent told me I would have been published by now if I'd been chosen. I had gotten my hopes up, so I felt a bit sad that they did not publish me. I supposed I needed to get used to this rejection if I was going to be auditioning again.

The next Monday morning, I dropped Lewis off at nursery like usual. When I got back home, my phone was ringing. It was my mother. When I picked up, she immediately started shouting at me, saying, "How could you do this?! It's cheap, how could you embarrass me?" And she slammed the phone down on me. I instantly knew what she was talking about. I ran down to the newsagent's across the street and picked up *The Sun* newspaper. I opened it up, and there I was spread across the whole page: "New Face" Zoë Paul. I had used Chris's last name to avoid a little disgrace and embarrassment to the Gregory family. I was topless in a pink swimming costume, smiling on Page 3.

I was ecstatic.

I ran home, and I didn't know what to do. I instantly called Chris, who was so happy for me. He was so proud of me. I felt overwhelmed, but I had to go to my parents' house to try to make things right. When I got there, my father opened the door. I walked in, and the newspaper was on the kitchen table. My mother was upstairs. My father said, "She is not happy with you at all. She doesn't even want to talk to you." My father couldn't even look me in the face. I didn't know what to do. I didn't know how to feel, so I left distraught. As I drove back to my flat, I felt happy and sad at the same time, not knowing whether to laugh or cry.

Had I been selfish in my decision? I was confused. I received mixed reactions from friends and family about the Page 3 publication, which made me distance myself from all of them.

The great thing was it did open a lot more opportunities for me in my career. I went on to shoot with Byron Newman, a talented photographer who worked for *Playboy* magazine. For *Playboy*, I shot alongside Katie Price, who was also a glamour model; we would become friends. We were both published in *Playboy's Book of Lingerie*; I remember seeing the pictures for the first time and thinking they were so beautiful. I was so proud of myself, and I was paid well for the shoot. I didn't really know much about the Playboy brand at the time, but through that experience, I learned it was a great company to work with.

My agent, Yvonne, would always have access to the best auditions.

For example, she got me an audition for a video game. With my look and fighting skills, I was chosen to play a fighting character in Sony PlayStation's *Fighting Force*, alongside model Kelly Brook. We went on tour to promote the game with Eidos Interactive at conventions in the US and UK. We had the most amazing character outfits that were custom made for us. It was one of the best jobs I had ever experienced as a model.

Kelly Brook and I in character for the Sony PlayStation game *Fighting Force*.

In time, my mother forgave me for what I had done in the newspaper, and we mended our relationship. I really needed her support and help with Lewis while I was going through this transition in my life.

CHAPTER 5

SUNSET

Because Chris was such a positive influence in my life, I trusted that he would have a great influence on my son as well. Once Lewis turned five, I felt he was old enough to soon meet Chris. We planned to take a holiday to Los Angeles. He wanted to make my dream come true by taking me to Hollywood, and I decided to bring my portfolio with me. I thought about visiting some modelling agencies whilst we were there.

The twelve-hour flight to Los Angeles was exhausting, but in front of me were the beautiful palm trees. The sun was shining when we landed. It was so hot. Los Angeles had a Western feel to it, with little wooden stores; it seemed a bit old-fashioned still. The atmosphere was relaxed. Everyone seemed to be happy and smiling in LA. Chris rented us a Mustang, a gorgeous sports car. It felt like a dream. This is what I had imagined as a child; the feeling was becoming a reality. We stayed on Sunset Boulevard, where all the excitement was. Los Angeles was alive.

On the third day of the trip, I went to see Otto Models on Sunset Boulevard. I met with Jason and Tereza Otto, who were so nice to me and very interested in sponsoring me. This would give me the chance to work in the states and in time relocate to Los Angeles permanently.

I got such positive feedback in Los Angeles; Tereza submitted me for a Guess campaign while I was sitting at her desk. I couldn't believe the kind of clientele she was submitting her models to.

Once we returned home to the UK, I started researching all the legalities involved with immigration and sponsorship. I felt apprehensive, eager, and curious. Could moving to LA possibly work? Would my son be happy? Would I miss my family? I didn't know the answers, but this was something I'd wanted since I was a child. I always knew this was a part of my destiny, a part of my future. It had to be the right thing to do because it made sense with all the dreams I'd had and wished for, and it seemed like all the dots were connecting.

Everything was moving so fast, but I was so ready for it.

Tereza from Otto models called me. They had prepared the paperwork for sponsorship. I had a phone meeting with Frank Ronzio, an immigration lawyer, about representing me. The meeting went well, and Frank wanted a retainer of $2,500 for me to hire him to start the paperwork. It was actually happening. It was going to come true. Chris was prepared to leave everything behind.

I kept my flat. I didn't want to give it up in case anything went wrong. I had told my mother and father that I'd be leaving for California and would call them once we got settled. Chris and I both sold our cars in the UK and packed up. Three weeks later, we left England for LA. We decided to book into a hotel in Hollywood, the Orchid Suites. The rooms were more like a studio apartment with a full kitchen. The hotel had a huge pool; we checked in and lived in the hotel for a couple of months until we found a beautiful condo to rent in West Hollywood.

A great school was close by for my son. I had registered him immediately with the school and local doctors. He seemed to be really happy; the condo we were renting had a beautiful pool that he wanted to play in every day, and right up the street was a hiking trail through Runyon Canyon, which was apparently Errol Flynn's old estate. The city was so beautiful. I had joined a local gym and started working out.

People in LA were so friendly, always saying hello or just talking to you as if they knew you; it was hard for me to get used to. In England, it is not like that. In fact, it's the complete opposite. My mentality was still on the streets of London; I still had the tough street-girl attitude. Quite often, people would try to talk to me in the gym, and I would tell them to fuck off. I didn't mean any harm, but that was the way of life that I was used to.

I knew I had to work on my aggression whilst being in LA and waiting for a work permit. I couldn't jeopardise this chance. I also knew I would be tested, just like I was on this beautiful summer's day.

My son and I were going shopping at Ralphs supermarket. I drove into the parking lot, and while I was waiting for another car to reverse out of a parking space, a speeding car cut into the parking spot that I was waiting for. They had seen me waiting for it. Lewis knew what was about to happen; I could see the fear in his face. He started to cry. I told him to stay in the car and lock the doors.

I lost my temper and got out of the car. I followed the two girls into the supermarket and got into a physical fight with both of them, beating both girls to the floor in the freezer aisle. Then I made a run for it. Lewis knew what had just happened. He saw the scratches on my face when I got back in the car.

I knew I had to stop getting myself into these situations, especially with my son around, and even more so while waiting for a work visa. I would get banned from the US for ten years if they arrested me for assault. I could get deported. I really had to work on myself from this point.

CHAPTER 6

RISKING IT ALL

Whilst waiting for my work visa, I received word from the lawyer that it would be delayed by a couple of months. Time was passing, and Chris and I were both unable to work legally. We were running out of money. Chris had some savings we were living on, and I was looking for jobs that paid cash to help with our living expenses, but that meant I'd be working illegally.

A friend introduced me to a photographer and filmmaker named Gary O. He told me about a project he was working on, a movie he was producing and would start filming very soon, and he asked if I was interested in taking a look at the script. I thought I should take the opportunity as we needed money, and it would be good for me since I had never tried real acting before. He booked me on the movie, which was going to film in Guatemala for a few days. The money was good, and it would be paid in cash, so I took the job. I had never even heard of Guatemala, but after doing some research, it sounded a little dangerous. At this point, though, I was willing to do pretty much anything I could to help with our living expenses.

We arrived in Guatemala. What a beautiful country. It really made me analyse a lot of things and gave me a great feeling of appreciation. I could see this was a poverty-stricken place, as so many children were begging on the street. I wanted to bring them all back to LA with me and take care of them.

On the day of filming, we were about to shoot a scene in the jungle. The scene required us to be totally naked and have fake weapons for a hostage scene. I was feeling a little wary about it, especially with all the bugs and things in the jungle.

We were in the middle of filming the scene when all of a sudden, we heard shouting. I couldn't understand what it was. The Guatemalan authorities and a jungle tribe suddenly ambushed us. They were pointing guns at us, telling us to put our weapons down; they thought we were some kind of terrorists shooting each other. I screamed, and everyone panicked and got down on the ground. I thought I was going to die, or we were going to jail; I thought they would hold us hostage. I thought I was going to get raped and they would kill me. They thought our weapons were real. I couldn't understand anything they were saying. I just kept my head down and prayed. Gary was trying to explain to them what we were doing.

Once the jungle tribe understood, everybody calmed down. They said we needed a permit to film on the land and asked if we had permission. They finally let us go; we didn't get to finish the scene, but we all just wanted to get the hell out of the jungle and get back to the villa. That was a surreal situation. I didn't really comprehend what danger we were in and how close I was to being shot dead.

After filming the movie, we returned to Los Angeles. We landed at LAX airport, where I was stopped by the Immigration and Naturalizaton Service (INS) and questioned about where I had been and what I was doing in Guatemala. They asked me so many questions: if I had been for pleasure, holiday, or working. They took me to the back, where I waited to be seen by a secondary immigration officer. I was so scared.

I had to deny everything: I told them I went for a holiday. The officers were tormenting me, recording everything I said. Chris was waiting outside to pick me up, but they would not let me use my phone to contact him. I didn't know what to do. I had an awful time in the INS secondary holding. They went through my Louis Vuitton Filofax, where I had notes in my diary. I had Polaroids from my topless Page 3 shoot. Unfortunately, they found my notes about the job I was filming in Guatemala, including the amount I was getting paid. They caught me. I should have known better than to have any trace of any work information. I had been caught working without a visa.

I knew I was going to be deported back to England; I could not believe what was happening. This was a nightmare. The officers handcuffed me and took me to a holding facility that was like a lockup jail close to the LAX airport, where I was held until the next flight back to England—that would be twelve hours later, the following day. I wasn't able to make any phone calls. There was no food or drinks available. All I could think about was my son, Lewis.

The next day, the officers escorted me through the airport in handcuffs; I felt so humiliated. They escorted me onto the airplane, still in handcuffs. The cuffs were taken off once I was in my seat. I had never been so embarrassed in my life.

Once I got back to the UK, I went to my grandmother's and contacted Chris and my lawyer, Frank Ronzio; I felt like my dream was crumbling before me. What about my son? Would I ever be able to go back to LA? What was I going to do? I was terrified, and

I was sure when my son found out, he would be devastated and so scared. I had no money with me and had not yet been paid for the movie. I had no idea what was about to happen.

My lawyer told me he needed a $3,500 retainer to start fighting this deportation case. He was quite sure we could get it done and get me back to LA in two months. I had to kick into survival mode; I went straight to Stringfellows nightclub, which featured exotic dancers. I auditioned, and two days later, I started work. I hated every moment of being an exotic dancer, but I was willing to do whatever it took to get back to my son. Within two weeks, I made the money we needed.

I called Lewis every day, and he would cry to me on the phone, telling me how much he missed me. It killed me to hear him say that to me. Two months passed; it was the longest eight weeks of my life. One morning, Chris called as usual, but this time with great news that the case was filed and approved, and the US had issued me my visa. I was able to return to Los Angeles.

It felt like I had won the lottery. The hardship had made me want the opportunity that much more. My determination and resilience paid off. I realised that karma had bitten me, and I had jeopardised a lot with such a poor decision. It was great to spend time with my grandmother while I was back in the UK, but I was so eager to return to LA.

I landed back at LAX, where I had to go to secondary again and explain the whole situation. I was being so nice to the immigration officers because I just wanted to be released, even though it was haunting to be back in that secondary room with the memories of how they had treated me. I had a flag on my passport, and I knew now I would probably go through this process every time I travelled internationally. I just couldn't wait to see my son. I was so emotional, happy, and relieved. I had never experienced anything like that, having my life torn apart, being taken away from my son, and feeling so helpless with nothing—no money, no resources.

I was back in LA and was now able to get a Social Security number, open a bank account, and get started with everything legitimately. Chris was still unable to work, since I was the only one with a visa, unless we were to get married. This is something we talked about, but it was for the reasons of the visa, not because of love. I was not ready to get married. Even if we were to get married, the filing and wait time for his visa would take at least eight months to a year and a half, so we had to find a way for him to work under my name and Social Security number.

We ended up going downtown and getting a marriage license, so we were prepared to apply for his Visa once mine came through.

Chris had a lot of contacts in LA, which made everything easier. He started DJing at the popular clubs in Hollywood, like The Gate and the Sunset Room. The checks were made out to me. He became the resident DJ and was doing really well and working consistently; I was back modelling and doing lots of TV. Filming TV commercials, I quickly learned that with my look, I would always be typecast as "the busty blonde."

Gary, who filmed the movie in Guatemala, introduced me to a talent manager, Robert Lombard. He would be holding a casting for a B-movie series for cable TV. I had no idea what B movies were. I went for a meeting with him, and he was a pleasant guy. He was confident that he could have me booked for work by the next day. He was a well-known manager in LA for casting B movies, erotic stories, adult TV, and cable series. I had expressed to him that I didn't want to do sexy movies or any porn. Robert was true to his word and had me booked the next day for a recurring role on a Cinemax cable show. I was working nearly every day, making good money, and I was being booked consistently. Robert had me working all the time on great mainstream commercials and got me great auditions for A-list movies. I starred alongside Dennis Hopper and Eric Roberts.

With Robert Lombard as my manager, I really became established in Los Angeles. I could have worked a lot more, but I started to resent the men I worked with in the B movies. They were, at times, unprofessional. Whilst shooting a simulated sex scene with me, they would get too excited, getting too aroused. I could feel it being rubbed up against me. I couldn't deal with the emotions involved, so I told Robert I didn't want to do any more B movies.

CHAPTER 7

THE PLAYBOY MANSION

While on set filming with my friend Tamie, she asked if I had plans that Sunday. She said she had an invitation to the Playboy Mansion pool party and asked if I would like to go. I absolutely took her up on the offer. I hadn't gotten around to contacting Playboy yet to let them know I was now living in LA. I told Chris that I had plans to go to the mansion and asked if he could babysit Lewis for a few hours. He was totally happy for me to go up there.

That Sunday, we drove to the mansion and approached the gates. A big rock contained a speaker intercom. Security asked for our names, and then the gates opened. We drove up a hill, where a valet took the car and said, "Have fun."

It was a big, beautiful house. I didn't know much about the mansion or what a big deal *Playboy* magazine was in America. It was picturesque. I had never seen anything so beautiful. With the sound of exotic birds chirping—as well as peacocks, parrots, monkeys, and bunny rabbits—it was like a living wonderland. A beautiful waterfall gushed from the mountain of rocks surrounding the pool and grotto. I didn't even know what a grotto was. There was a "Sunday fun day" menu, with food and snacks available to order.

I set eyes on Hugh Hefner, who was sitting on the other side of the pool, playing backgammon. I felt a little shy and in awe of this beautiful paradise. It was hedonism. Tamie and I grabbed a couple of lounge chairs to lie on and got into our bikinis.

Looking around, I was so curious about this big house. It looked like it had many rooms, lots of different pathways to different parts of the house, and trails into the gardens.

There were so many pretty girls everywhere. Girls were playing in the pool with pool toys. Some were at the pool bar with Playboy staff serving drinks. The girls were so pretty, their bodies so fit and perfect, the epitome of the real Barbie doll. Most resembled Pamela Anderson. I figured this was perhaps Hugh Hefner's type in women.

I felt like I just wanted to sit there all day and observe. It was so intriguing. I had a couple of cocktails, and I ordered a bite to eat from the menu. The servers would bring your order to you; it was such a pleasure to be catered to.

I spotted Hef getting up and walking towards where we were sitting; I thought perhaps he was going in the house. In any case, my heart started beating, and I got so nervous and starstruck. I was not ready for what was about to happen. He approached our lounge beds and stood there. He introduced himself, saying "Hi, I'm Hugh . . . and your name is?"

"Hi, I'm Zoë," I said.

He took a seat at the end of the lounge bed, and we continued talking. I mentioned I had just moved to LA from London, and that I had been shooting for *Playboy* in the UK. I thanked him for having us at the house and expressed my gratefulness for the hospitality.

He seemed curious about me; I could tell. He placed his hand on my knee and said, "I would like to invite you out to join us on Wednesday evening." He asked me for my phone number. He told me that he would have Mary take care of all the arrangements. I later found out that Mary was his full-time secretary. He took a Playboy pad and a pencil from the top pocket of the silk pyjamas he was wearing and passed it to me. "Write your number down," he said. I gave him my phone number, and then he said, "We will all have a great time," with a crafty, cheeky smile on his face.

I was so excited about the invite, and my mind started racing. Tamie and I talked about it for the rest of the day.

I later wandered around the grounds, discovering the underground gym that was equipped with everything, including tanning beds and beautiful open stone showers. I entered the grotto, which was like a cave. It had a small opening to enter and a little carved exit into the pool. Coupled with the grand waterfall, it was unreal. By the pool was a huge trampoline that the girls would jump and play on, along with lots of toys, like hula hoops, blow-up toys, frisbees, and volleyballs.

The peacocks walked around freely, as did the ducks and birds. There were bunny rabbits hopping in and out of the bushes. Around the back was a mini zoo, with birds, parrots, and monkeys. It was like a little jungle with cobblestone pathways leading to different areas of the grounds.

There was a separate game house that had unique arcade games and a pool table. It had two bedrooms, one with bouncy carpet, a TV, and a VHS player. The room was covered with mirrors. The game house had a mystique about it. *If these walls could talk*, I thought to myself; I felt good energy in there.

Outside on the grounds in the far back was a cute little white wishing well. Directly in front of the house was a grand water fountain with gorgeous lady statues and pretty flowers all around it. The estate was very well kept and included tennis courts as well as a separate guesthouse with three rooms. It was outstanding.

The place had a lot of charm and class, with so much character. It was rather dreamy. I felt serenity; I was excited about this place and about making contact with Hugh Hefner.

Once I returned home, I felt so full of joy—I couldn't believe what I had just experienced. The next morning, I woke up really excited and felt so motivated to get up and go to the gym and work out . . . if only I could use the gym at the mansion, and the sun beds, and spend the day there lying by the pool, talking to the animals.

CHAPTER 8

PARTYING WITH HEF

The next afternoon, I was on my way to pick up Lewis from school when my mobile phone rang. When I answered, a British voice said, "Zoë?"

"Yes," I said.

She continued, "This is Norma from the Playboy Mansion."

My heart began pounding. "Yes," I said, "how are you?"

Norma said, "Hef would like to invite you out with the girls on Wednesday night."

I didn't hesitate. "Of course," I said.

"We can send a limo for you."

I got a little nervous. I hate to be without my car and be stuck without a way to get home, so I said, "Oh, I can drive—that's no problem."

"That's fine. Get to the Playboy Mansion at 9:00 p.m. Drive onto the lot, and the valet will take care of your car. Your name will be on the list."

I was thrilled. This was so exciting to me—I couldn't wait till Wednesday! What was I going to wear? What about the other girls? So many things were going through my head.

I called my girlfriend Lana, whom I had modelled with in the past. I mentioned to her that I was going to go out with Hef and the girls on Wednesday, and funny enough, she said she was actually going too. I wondered why she hadn't mentioned it before or had not told me she had been attending the mansion pool parties. We would usually tell each other things like that and would invite one another, so I got the impression she wanted to keep it a secret. Or was she embarrassed about it, perhaps? I was a little confused. I knew I would see her soon and we would chat about it.

I wondered, *What do I say to Chris, even though I know he'll be fine with it?* He was being very supportive of this whole thing. It was such a buildup for me. I wanted to go buy a new outfit and really make an effort. This felt so right, and I was so lucky to have this opportunity.

I wished I could explain to Lewis what was going on. However, I didn't want to lie to him, so I didn't mention anything about it. And anyway, he would be asleep by the time I left for the mansion.

On Wednesday evening, after getting dressed and ready, I drove to the Playboy Mansion, making my way through Beverly Hills. It was a warm evening. It felt so surreal. I pulled up to the gate and waited, like the previous time. Then a voice came from the big rock. Security asked my name, and the gates opened. I had the biggest smile on my face driving up the hill to the house. I could hear the water fountain and the animals and birds singing. It was like a fairy tale. The valet took my car and was so polite and kind.

I got a little nervous as I walked into the house. It was quiet. In the dining room, a few girls were sitting, having drinks. They all turned around and looked at me in silence. Thank God Lana was there. I felt better once I saw her. I went and sat next to her, and we giggled at each other. I asked why she was hanging out with the Hef and the crew. I was asking question after question, but I felt better and more content that we were in this together. Finally, I didn't feel so shy around the other girls. I did feel a little tension from a couple of them, but Lana seemed to know them all, and that made everything easier for me.

One of the butlers walked out of the pantry and asked if I would like a drink. She was a pretty Black girl whom I instantly felt connected to. Carlina was her name. It felt like I had known her for years. It was weird. I had a drink of Malibu and pineapple. I was feeling a little more relaxed.

I was observing and listening to these girls and looking at what they wore; their outfits were rather outrageous and sexy. I felt a little underdressed and found myself already thinking about the next time I would go out with them and what I would wear. There was also talk about the Midsummer Night's Dream party that was coming up, and I really wanted to go. I was so curious about it.

When Hef came down the stairs, I felt a little intimidated. He walked into the dining room, and all the girls said hello to him. He walked over to me and said, "I'm happy to see you. I'm glad you could make it. We will have a lot of fun." He made me feel special. After taking some group pictures, we all made our way to the limo.

There were ten girls in total that night. I wasn't sure who his girlfriends were and who were just girls invited to go out. I was told that Tina Jordan was his number one, Tiffany Holiday was number two, and Holly Madison was number three. Holly was lucky to be hanging out, as she really wasn't what he was looking for, nor was she that attractive, but she was a girl who went along with anything just to be a part of the group. At first, I liked her.

There was another girl, named Bridget, who seemed to be Holly's friend. There were four girls who had been live-in girlfriends but had recently left the mansion; it was rumoured that they had been caught cheating, but I wasn't too sure. Other girls I met that night were Renee and Izabella. The others were girls shooting for the magazine and staying in the guesthouse; they would also come out and join the group.

When we got in the limo, it was decked out with drinks, champagne, snacks, sweets—anything you wanted. The music was loud, and everyone seemed to be having fun. We had a couple glasses of champagne on the way to the club, and I was feeling really good and quite tipsy by this point.

I loved that Hef wanted to take pictures of the group before we went into the club. We lined up with him to take a few pictures, and his own personal photographer snapped pics of us too. It was amusing to watch. People would stop and stare.

Hef's security then walked us into the club, where there was an area sectioned off for us, guarded by red velvet ropes. I quickly figured out there was a pecking order of the girls, a seniority regarding how the group would sit or who would be the closest to Hef.

I took a liking to Tina Jordan. She had a very sweet demeanour and a calming voice, and she seemed very sincere. She also had a child, so I could relate to her more. It was thrilling to see the people at the club stare at us. It was quite a sight to see Hugh Hefner and his entourage of blonde girls. It made me feel like a celebrity. I felt a premature sense of fame as I watched Hef dance the night away.

While we sat around the table, I saw Hef pass girls something. I was curious to know what it was, so I asked Tiffany. "Hey, Tiff? What is that he is giving out to the girls?"

"It's a quaalude," she said. "Do you want one?" I wasn't too sure what that was since we didn't have them in the UK. She explained what it was and the effects it gave: it would make one feel drunk without drinking—and make the whole night more enjoyable. "Try it," she said, nudging me with her arm, a big smile across her face.

Well, considering that unbeknownst to her, I knew all about drugs, I said, "Okay, yes, I would love to!" I hoped Hef would feel like I wanted to be involved and was willing to be a part of the group. I guess I was slightly manipulating the situation; I wanted him to see me as being fun and to make him happy, even if it meant being under the same influence as he was. I had so much fun that night—the quaalude was a good idea! Hef took a lot of pictures of all of us throughout the night.

Around 12:30 or 1:00 a.m., it was finally time to go. Security walked us back to the limo waiting right outside. One by one, we stumbled into the limo, laughing, giggling, grabbing snacks, making drinks, taking pictures.

We made our way back to the house, and everyone walked up the stairs towards Hef's room. I wasn't sure what I should do. I was concerned because no one had mentioned anything about when we all got back to the house.

I went to Lana and asked, "What happens now?"

Tina came over to me whilst I was asking Lana. Tina said, "Come to the room. We drink champagne and have strawberries and have a little fun."

I climbed the stairs with so many mixed emotions. I was scared, shy, and intimidated, as well as a little tipsy, but at the same time, I didn't want to ruin my chances for future invites to the parties.

When I got to the room, everyone jumped into the rectangular tile bath in Hef's main bathroom. All the girls seemed to be washing themselves, singing along with the music playing, and getting ready for the room. I joined in.

I was taking my time; I was so curious. I knew I was drunk, and I felt no inhibitions, nor was I thinking about anything but being in the moment. At one point, I thought to myself, "I should just act like I do when I'm shooting the B movies." I thought that mindset would get me through it. In retrospect, it was almost like I had been filming B movies specifically to prepare for this situation.

I walked from the bathroom into the bedroom; it was dark. I could hear voices and noises of sex. I could see a few girls lying down on the bed, watching two big TV screens that were playing pornographic movies. A couple of girls on the floor were pouring drinks. I sat with the girls on the floor; we were all naked.

I could hear a vibrating sound coming from the bed. I looked up to see what it was. All I could see were big vibrators. They actually looked like back massagers. The girls were using them as sex toys. I could hear all the erotic sounds, the sound of giggles and deep breaths. Above the bed on the celling was a huge mirror; I could see what was happening on the bed in the reflection. I looked around his room, which was cluttered with books, videos, stuffed animals, pictures, and gifts he'd accumulated over the years. It had a mystique to it. I could almost feel the scandalous adventures played out in the past in this room. The chandelier was covered with women's thongs. I was going to make sure I hung mine up there at the end of the night.

Tina called me onto the bed and told me to lie next to her. She passed me a vibrator and pointed to the wall outlet to plug it in, so I did. At first, I didn't make contact with the vibrator. I wasn't sure if it was clean or who had used it before me. Tina assured me all the toys were cleaned. She was very reassuring and watched over me more so than the other girls. I enjoyed watching her with Hef. She had a unique bond with Hef; he was infatuated with her. I liked the love they had for one another.

Everyone was sexually aroused and fondling one another, though whether it was all for show or it was real, I couldn't tell yet. A joint of weed was being passed around from one girl to the next. Hef was enjoying the show. Girls would take turns with Hef and intermingling with each other. It was a light orgy, nothing gruesome at all. It was a sexual playground, and because I was drunk, I went with the flow and joined in with the group. It was all new to me. I hadn't ever had group sex before, but I felt okay with it. One by one, each girl would straddle him and thrust on him for a couple of minutes, until the next girl would take her turn. I didn't have sex with Hef that night. He finished himself off, and then all the girls scattered to the bathroom, washing the vibrators, talking, giggling. I have to say it was a fun group of girls. I particularly bonded with Tina that night—we giggled so much.

I cleaned myself up, got my stuff, called for my car, and took off home. The drive home was gruelling, with so many things going through my head. It was exciting but emotional. Was I going to tell Chris everything that had happened? I decided not to because I didn't have intercourse. I just fondled and engaged in foreplay. I justified it to myself and kept silent.

Friday was another going out night for Hef and the girls. I had received the call from Norma, another of Hef's secretaries, and I was going out with the group again. I had time to think about everything and what part I wanted to play. This time, I made more of an effort with my style of clothing, and I was prepared for everything that was involved in the night. When I arrived at the mansion, Hef was giving out packs of photographs from our previous night out and gave me one too. I was ecstatic that I had some sort of memorabilia of this wonderful experience. I felt so lucky.

Friday was a repeat of Wednesday, and then Sunday pool day was during the weekend. Hef asked me to attend and stay for movie night on Sunday. I wasn't sure what that meant, but Tina again reassured me. It felt great that I could trust Tina; she was very nurturing and honest. Sunday pool day at the mansion was a lot of fun. There would be a lot more girls—random girls this time, quite a few of whom would try to get in on the party group night out, but most of the girls who came on Sunday were pool fillers, nothing more. I felt rather privileged at this point to be part of the going out group.

Hef would play backgammon with friends in the back of the garden, and we would lie out on the beds next to him and order food and drinks. I was getting to know the other girls by this time; to be honest, they were not the type of girls I grew up with, so I found myself adjusting a little. They were not rough around the edges like my old friends in the UK, and they didn't seem to have deep intellectual conversations. I seemed to get along with all of them, though the chatter was small talk and a lot of giggling. It almost seemed fake. I took a liking to all the staff at the mansion. They were so professional, polite, and welcoming. I absolutely loved the butlers and security, as well as the zookeepers and cleaners. They had all been there for a while. I built such a rapport with them all. I would always joke and be playful when I talked to them.

I was sunbathing when Hef came over and sat on the bed I was lying on. He asked if I was having a nice time. He asked me about my living situation and said he would like it if I would spend more time at the mansion. I was delighted and surprised, but I hadn't told him about Chris yet—and didn't know if I was even going to tell him at all.

And what about Lewis? I had told Tina that I had a son, and I was certain she would mention it to Hef at some point. The brilliant thing was I had learned that Hef's ex-wife lived next door with their two sons, Marston and Cooper, who happened to be the same age as my son. I remember thinking to myself that if I continued spending time at the mansion, then at some point I could perhaps bring my son along and introduce him to Hef's sons. Tina had her daughter at the mansion a lot; Hef's sons were over at the mansion a lot too. I loved that it was a family-oriented unit. I told Hef that I had an apartment in Hollywood, and he asked if my son lived with me. I had had a feeling he already knew! It took an enormous weight off my chest; I had been dreading telling him.

CHAPTER 9

THE GIRLS

I had mentioned to Hef that I had a gorgeous model friend, Sheila, whom I thought he would love. She reminded me of Kimberley Hefner, Hef's ex-wife. I was hoping perhaps we could invite her out on the next going out night. He was all for it! I was jumping the gun, but I found myself thinking to the future and that possibly Sheila would be in this with me, having this experience with me. I felt very confident that Hef was going to love Sheila, and it would take a lot of focus off me, as I still had a family at home and knew I wasn't able to commit to Hef 100 percent like I wanted to. If Hef took a liking to Sheila, it would perhaps double my chances for a solid position in the group, and I knew Sheila would never take my position or move forward without me. So I persuaded her to make this work.

Sheila came out with us, and Hef couldn't take his eyes off of her. Hef and Sheila had amazing chemistry as soon as I introduced them. I had predicted this, and it was all going to plan. The other girls were pleasant towards her. Sheila is a very likable person with an outgoing personality. We had a lot in common and were very much alike. She looked up to me as a big sister even though she was older than me. She soon became a part of the party posse. It was more fun now that I had a close friend by my side. We would plan our outfits and be excited together. I felt like she genuinely started to have feelings for Hef, and it was so lovely to watch them bond.

Sheila, Hef, Tina, and me.

As I spent more time at the mansion, it became evident to me that Tina was in the last days of her relationship with Hef. I knew Hef would be devastated if Tina left, but I could feel something in the air. Tina started to miss our going out nights and began spending more time at her home with her daughter. Tina was entitled to two nights off a week to spend time with her daughter and was the only girlfriend who was ever given nights off away from the mansion. She was Hef's number one girl; she shared the main room with Hef, so he would sleep alone two nights a week.

Tina was pushing for me to move into the mansion. She would always mention to Hef how much she liked me. I felt like she wanted to leave and wanted me to distract him from what was about to happen. At this point, if anything was going to happen, like Tina leaving, there was a whole group—me, Sheila, Renee, Izabella, Lana, and Bridget—to keep him happy, but I had built up such a great bond with Tina that I was sad to think she might take off. She had all the rules at the mansion down to a fine science, and Sheila, Iz, Renee, Lana, Tiffany, and I wondered whether things would change if she left—and who was going to take her place as the number one girl. I knew Tiff didn't want to, and neither did I. I couldn't, especially with my situation at home.

The only one who seemed to be hopelessly devoted was the black swan, Holly. The next time we went out, some new girls joined us, none of whom seemed to have a chance with Hef as a girlfriend. I found myself being a little territorial, but that night, Holly instantly made friends with one of them. Holly was a loner, and no one really liked her. By this point, we all just tolerated her. She just wasn't interesting and had nothing relevant to say, but she found comfort in dressing up as Hef's favourite movie stars. I have never been one to grovel. If a girl won't make the effort with me, I won't entertain a fake friendship, so Holly and I just tolerated each other. I had Lana, Sheila, and Iz in my little group, and I felt like we had a clique of a tight friendship.

Tiffany, number two, was very bubbly and always smiling. She was actually quite eccentric. She liked rhinestones, pink feathers, and glitter. She was confident with her sexuality and always a great performer in the bedroom. We got along great, but I was still a little rougher around the edges than she was. Lana and Tiffany had the most in common. They both had a little rockstar edge, wearing grungy clothing with studs and leather. I had known Lana for a while from doing modelling projects together. People would often think we were sisters, as we looked a lot alike. I found out Lana had been going out with the group a couple of months prior to me coming along, but she'd kept that a secret. She was on and off with her boyfriend at the time, but I also felt like she was ashamed to be one of the Playboy group girls.

Iz was a little reserved. She was studying to become a lawyer at the time and also had a boyfriend she'd been dating for a few years. We laughed a lot together. She was willing to take a puff of a joint with me and laugh in hysterics. She made fun of how I pronounced things with my Cockney British accent. She was more opinionated than I was and liked a good argument. I always wondered what she was doing in this situation when she had been to university and wanted to be a lawyer. I thought she had so much more going for here than to be in Hef's entourage.

Renee was sweet. She reminded me of Tina. I enjoyed her company. She was fun, always up for anything. Renee was a friend of Tina's and also had a daughter. Tina had introduced her to the group. Sheila and Renee got on really well. She was very well organised and appeared to be a good mother. I liked that about her.

Tina finally had the talk with me that I was so dreading. I loved Tina so much, and so did Hef. I was devastated to hear she had decided to leave and spend more time with her daughter, but I had to respect that. She asked me if I would consider moving into the mansion and said she thought Hef would like it. I told Tina I would think about it.

By now, Holly was always by Hef's side when Tina was gone with her daughter. It seemed that Holly was taking over Tina's role. She was willing to watch silent movies with him during the week;

she was always there for him, and I thought that was good for Hef. She took an interest in everything Hef did and always did her homework on things that he was into. I was never sure whether her interest was genuine or she was strategically making the right moves to wiggle her way to the top. It caught my attention that she was becoming territorial over Hef, and that was fine with the rest of us, as we didn't have an agenda to become Hef's number one.

CHAPTER 10

HOME SWEET HOME

The party posse was now a consistent group. Wednesdays and Friday, we'd go out and then return to the mansion for a rendezvous. Sunday fun day meant all day by the pool, then a group dinner with some of Hef's close friends, some of whom had been coming to the mansion for years. We'd watch a premiere of a new movie release in the movie room around 7:00 p.m., and then Iz, Lana, Renee, Sheila, and I would go home. It was good to get used to the routine; it gave us insight into what it would be like to move into the mansion and what the schedule was.

I wanted to get to know Hef better, but it was hard to get his attention or be alone with him. I was happy to become a regular, and he was pleased with what I was offering. Those of us not living there yet would often talk about moving into the mansion. Even though it had never come up in conversation with Hef, Tina who was already living in the house, had been hinting that since the previous girls had left, there were vacancies. We asked one another if we had intentions to move in.

I needed to find out a lot more about what was involved in moving in and what was expected. With the chatter between us girls, we had decided if it was going to happen, we would all do it together.

I suppose I had decided that I wanted to move in, and now I had to figure out how I was going to approach my home situation. During the time I had been spending at the mansion, Chris and I had become distant, but we were still on good terms. I had to sit down and talk to him—and try to come up with the best way to make it work with my son. I think Chris knew all along that it was going to come to this, and he supported me. He also knew what a big deal it was, and he never wanted to hold me back if it's what I wanted to do.

It seemed easy enough when I thought about it. My son would stay at my apartment during the week and possibly stay with me at the weekends at the mansion. When I talked with Chris about it, he was all for it. I had planned it out in my head that I would stay at the mansion, pick up my son from school every day during the week like I always did, do school homework at home, cook like I always had, and put him to bed. Then, I would return to the mansion once he was asleep. I would tell him that I had to work night shifts at my job. Before I could commit to moving in, I would have to make sure my son was going to be able to come to the mansion and be a part of my other life. It all seemed like it could work.

I was eager to find out about the house rules and what kind of commitment was expected. I gathered all the information I could. I asked the butlers and Tiffany. Eventually I asked Mary, Hef's main secretary, as she had all the answers about everything. Mary was rather stern and had an authoritative demeanour about her. I was a little intimidated by her. It was rumoured that the girls would get a weekly allowance, a car payment and possibly a new car, health insurance, a dress allowance for all party outfits, and cosmetic surgery. There was a curfew of 9:00 p.m. for all girls to be home, and they could never be late. No one was to have a boyfriend. It was rumoured that Hef would have private investigators follow you if he had any indication of cheating.

Bedrooms three, four, five, and six were vacant in the mansion. I figured Bridget had become so close with Holly that she would take room three, which was the biggest room and had three beds. I did not want to share a room with anyone. I was kind of hoping she would be the one to take room three. I liked room four, as it looked over the pool area. It was on the second floor at the back corner of the house, but it had a shared bathroom with room five, so I wanted to make sure whoever took room five was a good friend of mine. I wanted Lana to have it, as I was still getting to know Izabella and we were still trying to click. Sheila wasn't ready to move in, but I knew it wouldn't be long before she did. Hef couldn't leave her alone; he adored her.

I went to Tina and hinted my thoughts on the moving-in situation, knowing she would say something to Hef. In that way, the seed was planted about the room idea. We girls had already claimed the rooms we liked when we were talking about it. It was going to work out nicely, if Bridget would commit to room three. Everyone was getting along great, and there was excitement in the house with the way things were progressing with the group. Even though it was early days, there was harmony between us all. Hef seemed happy too.

Tiffany had mentioned that if we did move in, we could decorate our rooms how we wanted, have them painted, get new bedding, and so on. I was really excited about that.

Lewis overheard my conversations with Chris about everything going on. He was aware of what was happening, and I wanted to take him to the mansion to see for himself. I asked Hef if it was okay to bring my son with me on a weekend, perhaps on a Saturday. He was happy to have Lewis come. Hef's sons would also be on the Playboy grounds. Marston and Cooper were cool kids. I always saw them when I was at the mansion. They would come in and out, having fun and being adventurous, and I knew Lewis would love to hang out with them. I was excited for Lewis.

Saturday came, and we made our way through Beverly Hills. Lewis turned to me and said, "This looks like a nice area, Mum."

I smiled at him and said, "You haven't seen nothing yet."

When we pulled up to the rock, security already knew it was me. They said through the speaker, "Welcome back, Zoë." Lewis thought that was so cool. We drove up, and Lewis's face was so surprised. He saw a peacock walking around and couldn't believe his eyes. Going to the mansion was still like a dream to me also. Just seeing the look on his face made me feel so thankful; I realised how fortunate we were.

The valet took my car, and Lewis was standing there just looking around. He was a little quiet, probably just surprised with excitement. We walked through the house to the back and walked outside to where the animals and pool were. He was extremely excited when he saw the trampoline, and he immediately wanted to get on it.

A couple of the butlers came over and introduced themselves to Lewis. They were quite shocked I had a son, and they instantly took a liking to him. All the butlers were so nice. I was becoming very close with a few of them, more so than most of the other girls. Lewis didn't hesitate to get into the pool. He went on to order some food that turned out to be the best he'd had in a long time. He was so happy and loved every minute of it.

A little while later, Marston and Cooper appeared. Right away, they came over and said hi to Lewis. They wanted him to go and play with them; I was a bit worried, but I wanted them to make friends right away, so off they went. I didn't see Lewis for a couple of hours. I stayed by the pool, lying in the sun. The butlers were keeping an eye on the boys, which made me feel a lot better. I texted Chris and told him Lewis has already gone off with the boys. We figured it wouldn't take long for them to make friends. Renee wanted to bring her daughter to the mansion too. It was so nice that Hef was okay with us bringing our kids to be involved in this experience.

Lewis and Cooper Hefner.

When the boys returned a few hours later, Cooper asked me, "When will Lewis be coming back?" How sweet he was—I was actually so relieved that he had said that, and it seemed they had all got along really well. Lewis didn't want to leave and asked if we could stay a bit longer, so we stayed till around 7:00 in the evening. I was ecstatic that the boys were having so much fun. It was important for Lewis to feel comfortable, too, if we wanted to have a life at the mansion.

I knew that on Sunday I would be expected to be at the mansion for the regular Sunday fun day by the pool, followed by dinner and a movie in the evening, but I really wanted Lewis to come meet the other girls and some of the other people I knew would be attending. I would have to ask Hef, as I knew Mary was not working on Sunday. Hef was in the scrap room, working on his scrapbooks at the time, and I didn't want to disturb him. I decided that I'd call him from home later on and ask, which would be my first time actually calling the mansion and asking to speak to Hef. I didn't know if that would be possible, but I wanted to try. I was really surprised when he took my phone call. I hated to bother such a busy man, but it needed to happen. Hef said Lewis was welcome anytime. Hef made me so happy that day, giving me this feeling that everything was falling into place.

Since everything with Lewis was arranged, I felt no more hesitation about moving into the mansion.

I moved into room four, overlooking the back of the estate where the pool and grotto were. Lana was in room five next to me. Bridget, Holly, and Renee all went into room three, and Iz was in six. The schedule pretty much remained the same; I would always work out in the morning and then lie by the pool for a while. It was therapeutic for me, and I was absorbing it all in every day. I would feel so chuffed and grateful for where I was in the present moment.

Lying by the pool at the mansion and talking to Gus the Goose.

CHAPTER 11

LIVING MY DREAM

Tina was finally moving out, and her departure really affected Hef. For a while, the mood was sombre in the house, but all we could do was try to cheer Hef up by having as much fun as possible.

There was a domino effect of each girl getting plastic surgery. First it was Holly—she needed it—then me, then Lana, then Iz. I suppose that part of the rumour was true, Garth Fisher was the surgeon to Hef's girls. Between the nose jobs and boob jobs, Garth did pretty well over all the years of Hef's girlfriends.

It took some time for Hef to get over Tina. Holly continuously tried moving into Hef's room, but he wasn't ready for it. He would get angry with her when he would find her things in the closet. I guess she was secretly going into his room and putting her stuff in there. Over the course of a few weeks, though, he finally allowed Holly to move into his room permanently.

I felt like once Holly was with Hef as his main girlfriend, her attitude changed towards the rest of us. She acted like she had seniority, and she started to try to manipulate Hef into believing the bullshit she would make up about us girls—especially about me, because I was the rebel and an easy target. She created stories about me that I was being mean to her. It was the start of the friction she would cause within the group.

The other girls saw the moves Holly was making and began to side with me. We were the A-Team. I think because we all moved in together, we had a pact. The B-Team was Holly and Bridget. Tiffany stayed neutral.

A team.

I had no problem asking Hef for surgery, a new car, or whatever I wanted, and that was because of how Tina had guided me. This was a job to me, and I wanted to look my best to represent the

Playboy company. Tina had also told me how much Hef liked me, so I felt secure in my position. I had to think smart whilst given this opportunity, and as I could see there were others already trying to sabotage me, I needed to start saving my wages. I needed to apply for a green card when my visa ran out in nine months, so I had to save and not go shopping like the other girls. Yes, it was a bit frustrating for me. I would watch the girls come home from shopping on Rodeo Drive in Beverly Hills, with new shoes, bags, and clothes. But I had to think about Lewis and our future. I wanted to remain in the United States, so I needed a green card. That was my priority. I got a safe deposit box at Bank of America, and I would take my pay every week from working at the mansion and stash it there. I didn't want to deposit cash in the bank.

The only thing I was worried about was I had not paid any taxes for the first year I had been in the States legally. I needed to take care of the issue; I just didn't know where to start, as Chris had previously had all the checks made out in my name from his DJing gigs. I felt like it was going to present me with a problem, so I was avoiding it.

I spoke to Hef and Norma in the office about my visa situation and said I needed to apply for a green card soon, but I would need some help with some letters of recommendation from reputable companies and people. I felt like he was the only one who was capable of helping me, as he knew everyone. I wanted to get the ball rolling as soon as I could. I knew the process would take a long time, and I didn't want to have to go back to the UK or be deported again. Hef actually suggested I talk to his lawyers to see what it would involve and what was needed. I contacted his law firm, Baker McKenzie, and we started to get things in order to prepare for filing. I was ready to pay for the retainer, but I had to persuade the lawyers that it was me paying for it and I didn't have Hef's budget. Everything was looking possible—with all the credits I had from previous modelling and acting work, and with all the help from Hef, it was looking good. We filed, and now we just had to wait; I was also waiting to receive the bill for the retainer from Norma, Hef's secretary.

Some time went by, and I contacted the lawyer regarding billing, as I wanted to get it paid for. I didn't want all that money sitting in the bank. On the call, the lawyer told me that Hef had taken care of it. I was speechless. I couldn't breathe. I couldn't believe it. I ran to the office to speak to Norma, and she confirmed it had been taken care of. I still can't believe Hef did that for me. I never expected it. No one had ever been so kind to me in my life. I wanted to know how much it was, but Norma said, "It's better that you don't." I was baffled. So I left it at that, but I knew I could obtain the information from the lawyer. I needed all the paperwork for my records. I was on cloud nine, so high on life. How was I so lucky? What an amazing human being Hef was. Getting a green card was like winning the lottery to me, and I wanted it so badly. I could never have done it by myself or afforded it without a couple of consistent jobs. Hef made it happen—he set me up for my future, for my son's future. He had changed my life. That is how it felt. Hef became my ultimate hero.

I didn't want to tell any of the girls, and I had asked Hef and Norma to keep it to themselves until the application was approved. I didn't trust anyone, and I sure didn't want anyone trying to sabotage it for me. I didn't want to take the risk of them getting jealous because Hef was helping me with such a major deal.

I woke up the next morning, and something hit me: I was still married to Chris! How was this going to affect the green card? Hef didn't know I was married! I started to panic. I didn't know what to do. I'm sure within the paperwork it had to have asked about my marital status. Did it say I was single? What was I to do? I had to think; I had to strategise my next move. How was I going to handle this? I would have to call the lawyer and explain it to him. I decided not to say anything to Norma or Hef; I had to try to convince the lawyer not to mention anything or forward any updated paperwork, or this was not going to happen. The lawyer wouldn't get his payday, and I wouldn't get my green card—and neither of us should jeopardise that. He was smart enough to agree. That was probably one of the most stressful days of my life.

Even though we made an agreement not to alert anyone else, I was still on eggshells every day. Iz and I went shopping for new cars, and I decided to get a used car and finance it, so I wouldn't owe much in case anything went wrong with my situation. Iz decided to go with a new one. I got a black Land Rover Discovery, fit for my Lewis and his bike, surfboards, and other stuff; I had to be practical. Our mansion limo driver, Freddy, had great contacts for rims, wheels, and upgrades for our cars. We purchased new twenty-four-inch rims and made our cars look fancy. It was the first car I had that I was proud of.

Hef was such a generous man. I had never been so spoiled. I would often look back at my life and realise how far I had come.

But even though I was feeling happy and lucky, things weren't so great for everyone in the house. I hadn't seen Tiffany for a couple of days or seen her car outside. Something felt off; I went to the pantry to talk to the butlers and ask if they had seen Tiff. One of them told me that something had happened with Tiff and Hef, and she was moving out. Tiff had lived at the mansion for a couple of years prior to my moving in. I had only been living there for six months, and now she got kicked out? I needed to find out what happened.

No one seemed to know why, or maybe they did but didn't want to say anything to me. It was the last thing I saw coming. I didn't know of any drama going on. It was so sudden, but I did know that Tiffany had had an apartment in Hollywood for a while. I had been there a few times with her, so I knew she would be fine with her living situation. Still to this day, I don't 100 percent know the whole truth, but after I had inquired with the rest of the girls, I gathered that Tiffany seemed to think I had something to do with it and that I wanted her out. Maybe Holly put that idea in Tiff's head; Holly was targeting me again because we were not getting along. She was always up to her tricks, a repetitive behaviour—it was evident that she didn't like me at all.

I have to say even though I favoured some girls over others, every single one of them threw me under the bus at some point while I was there at the mansion, all of which I knew about. I never acted upon knowing the other girls were telling tales on me. I had to think smart and be patient while I was waiting for the green card.

I called Sheila and told her to come out with us on Wednesday. I also told her about Tiff getting kicked out and how this would be the perfect opportunity to move into the house. I really wanted her there, as she was my friend and Hef loved her. She was favourable to our A-Team, and having Sheila in the house as my best friend would take a little heat off of me. Sheila would do anything I told her, and Hef knew that. I convinced her to move in; she took my room four, and I moved into Tiff's old room. Now I was Hef's number two girl.

It's crazy how the dynamics worked, Holly on one side of him and me on the other. We hated each other at this point; you could see it in all the group pictures we took. The look on her face says it all, and from the look on mine, you can see I'm not too bothered—ha!

Having Sheila at the house brought a lot more positivity; I hadn't seen Hef this happy since Tina was there. Sheila got along with everyone. She actually brought Hef and me closer, and that's what I needed to happen. We had some major events coming up: we attended the Grammys and the AFI Awards, and we took the private jet to New York for the fiftieth anniversary of *Playboy*. We attended many events, and we were constantly on TV and captured by the paparazzi while out and about or during parties at the mansion.

Sometimes, other companies would rent out the back of the mansion to hold parties too. We were not supposed to attend them, but we did anyway. We would go to Sheila's room, where we could see out back and see who was there. We would always see celebrities and very famous people. We'd sneak out and run down to try to get our picture taken with them. We were not supposed to be out in the back. The butlers never told on us, but security would sometimes catch us and report us to Hef.

CHAPTER 12

FIRST CHRISTMAS WITH HEF

Christmas was coming, and I had no idea what to give a man who had everything. But I did know it was going to be a great Christmas. Lewis was going to be with me to celebrate, and I was finally in a position to give him anything he wanted—and I did. It made me so happy and fulfilled to finally have the freedom I'd never had before to make my son the happiest kid on earth. I couldn't wait.

Hef had given all the girls money to buy gifts for one another. I thought that was so sweet of him. I probably would have despised spending my own money on the girls, especially the girls I didn't like. Having a budget from him made everything so much easier for me.

Christmastime in the mansion felt magical. Christmas songs were playing, the decorations were extravagant, and a feeling of joy was in the air. While in the office talking with Norma, I watched stacks of Christmas cards flooding in from all over the world by the hundreds. So many people sent Hef gifts; the office was crammed with so much stuff. We were invited to a couple of Christmas parties in Holmby Hills, where the mansion was. Across the street from the mansion lived Jimmy Iovine and Nicolas Cage, and we attended both of their parties; it was so convenient that we could walk across the street to them. We took a trip to Malibu to see Diana Ross at her beach mansion. That's where I met all of her children.

Kimberley, Hef's ex-wife who lived next door to the mansion, invited Lewis and me for dinner on Christmas Day; I thought that was very nice of her, though I couldn't figure out whether she was trying to get close to me for info or it was genuine. Only time would tell. But a couple of the girls got a little jealous about my closeness with Kimberley—I'm sure only because they knew she took a liking to me and would put in good words to Hef on my behalf.

Izabella, Lana, and I decided to do a nude photo shoot and get a group picture of all of us together for Hef's Christmas present. We gave him two different pictures. They turned out amazing! I had them framed in big, classic, gold frames. I wasn't into giving stuffed teddy bears and useless things like ornaments; he already had tons of junk in his room that he had accumulated over the years. But behind his bed on the shelf, he kept the pictures of his girlfriends, and that was the purpose of the shoot. This way, he would have a professional picture of his three prettiest girls on that mantelpiece. I had the picture made into an eight-by-ten and professionally framed, not a four-by-six like the other girls had given him. This was eye-catching. I couldn't wait to give it to him.

On Christmas Day, Lewis stayed at the mansion with me. I had given him some gifts there and saved some at the apartment for him, so we could have a Christmas with Chris the next day as well. Lewis called Marston and Cooper next door; he wanted to go over and play with them.

I was rather excited for my first Christmas at the mansion, though I wasn't sure what to expect. The mansion staff were preparing for the big dinner in the afternoon with some of Hef's closest friends and other guests, most of whom were his age and had been attending the same Christmas party at the mansion for years. It was to be a grand dinner followed by a Christmas movie.

In the afternoon, we were summoned to Hef's room to open gifts. We were all so excited! For the one hour we were all together opening gifts, all the resentment went away—or at least we all acted like it did. We all had to fake being thankful to one another in front of Hef for the gifts we got each other. Hef just wanted harmony, and that's what I did my best to deliver him.

It must be hard to give seven girls different gifts of their preference, so I assumed we would all get the same things, and I was right. We opened our gifts from Hef: we got Playboy clothing, Playboy jewellery, Playboy everything—art, books, bits and pieces. We also received money on top of our regular weekly allowance.

Then it was Hef's turn. He opened his pictures, and he loved them. It was actually great to see Holly and Bridget's faces; they were so jealous, but they had to say how awesome the pictures were in front of Hef. I got a kick out of that. Ha!

When we had finished with gifts and gone back to our rooms, I called Kimberley Hefner. I told her Lewis and I would pop over but would not stay for dinner, as dinner at the mansion was around the same time, and we were to be there. I found it really enlightening that Kimberley took a liking to me. I'm not sure how I would feel under the circumstances, being friends with one of the seven girlfriends of my ex-husband. She would always talk sense to me, asking about my future and what I was going to do after the mansion. She would say, "The mansion situation won't last forever." I would leave Kimberley's house thinking about the things we talked about. I listened to everything she said. She had been around this situation and seen what it was like for so many years, so I needed to pay attention and take her advice. I also wanted Lewis to continue his friendships with the boys in the future, no matter what happened. I wanted them to remain friends because I was sure the Hefner boys would one day grow up with a legacy to follow, and perhaps they would take over the Playboy company.

Kimberley loved my Lewis; he was such a good boy. The butlers told me the other boys would end up getting Lewis into trouble. The boys were always up to mischief, and the butlers would catch them but not tell on them, not wanting to jeopardise the boys' freedom at the mansion.

Getting ready for Christmas dinner, Izabella and I had fun guessing what the other two girls were going to wear. They always went over the top with outfits to try to impress Hef, but it would usually end in them being laughed at. It was hilarious. Sometimes Holly would come down to dinner in a mini satin dressing gown and hair done like Marilyn Monroe, with no underwear. It was pathetic. I was so embarrassed for her. You could see people around the table eyeing each other and putting their heads down, trying not to laugh.

The food was always so good; the kitchen cook was amazing. I couldn't wait till dinner, so I went to the pantry to see the butlers and the cooks and wish them a merry Christmas. I went into the kitchen to take a look and taste the food. It was amazing. I couldn't wait to eat. I liked to taste the food in front of the cook so he could see the satisfaction on my face. Yes, I was very friendly with all staff at the mansion; they loved it, and it kept everyone in a great mood.

Iz and me being goofy at the table, trying to ignore the stupidity
of the other girls.

Dinner at the table with the group was becoming more difficult.
It was mandatory to have dinner together at 6:00 p.m. on Sundays
and holidays, but it was difficult to listen to some of the girls talk
nonsense and have nothing interesting to say. I felt like that was
why they dressed up: to try to make themselves interesting. Iz and I
would constantly be nudging each other under the table and burst-
ing into laughter. It was painfully funny, and the butlers were in on
it too. I would smoke some weed before dinner to make it a little
easier to deal with stupidity.

Lewis and I had a second Christmas at home at our apartment
with Chris. I felt guilty about spending Christmas Day away from
him, but he knew it was work, and in order to get my allowance, I
had to be there.

CHAPTER 13

HUSTLING

O nce Christmas was over and the New Year came, I was patiently waiting to receive my green card. I knew I had to keep the peace and wait it out. I was thinking ahead. Once I had my green card, I could buy a condo. I had saved quite a lot of money working at the mansion. I would save my allowance every week, along with my party outfit allowance. It was all in cash in my safe deposit box at the bank. I knew if I was going to buy a condo, I would need to pay at least a couple of years' worth of back taxes.

While living at the mansion, I had been doing some consistent modelling work, but I would need to declare that I had earnings in cash too, in order to demonstrate that I could afford a mortgage. I started depositing some money in the bank to show that I was consistently working and getting wages. I asked Norma about the money we received for our work allowance, and she told me Hef had already paid taxes on it, so I didn't have to worry about that.

I needed to talk to Chris about depositing his DJing checks in my account. I didn't want to be solely responsible for the taxes, but I was planning ahead. I started that process. So I paid taxes for the previous two years I had been working at the mansion and started depositing cash into my account, hoping by the time my green card came, my bank account would be looking up to par. I was making sure I would have at least the 3 percent down payment to buy a condo and get a loan. I was still helping Chris with the rent at my apartment in Hollywood too.

Every Sunday, I would look in the newspaper to get an idea of what real estate prices were in Hollywood. I found it exciting just to think of owning my first home, something I had worked hard for, even though I didn't feel like I was working at the mansion. The feeling of gratitude overwhelmed me. I really cherished Hef during these moments. Being in this man's life was making all of my dreams come true.

Everything was going well at the mansion. I would wake up every day, have breakfast, work out, visit all the animals, and then lie by the pool and smile, feeling so happy.

I spoke to my mum every couple of weeks, but I didn't tell her everything that was going on. I didn't want to disappoint her any more than I already had, so I just told her that everything was progressing and Lewis and I were very happy. She gave me news of my brother having kids and kept me up to date with everything. She also told me she had split from my father, and that really crushed me. She didn't sound unhappy; she sounded relieved of the matter. She talked about coming to visit me soon, and I was ecstatic at the thought. I wanted to make her so proud of me.

CHAPTER 14

TEMPTATION

The mansion often held boxing events and the occasional after party for X Games, golfing, and tennis tournaments. We were all big fans of boxing and would always be present for the live events. The athletes would be in their trailers on the mansion grounds.

At one point, when the mansion was hosting a boxing match, one of the butlers mentioned that one of the fighters was from England and asked if I knew him. I did not know him personally but had heard of him. I was intrigued. My bedroom windows looked out to the front of the grounds where the trailers were. I had the chance to check all the boxers out while they were preparing for the matches.

Once we were all sitting around the boxing ring, the announcer introduced the boxer and his opponent: David Haye versus Vance Winn. The fight didn't last long. The British boxer, David, won that fight; he came over to meet Hef, and that's when we locked eyes.

He returned to his trailer, and I ran back to my room to watch him from my window. When he came back out, I ran downstairs and then walked out to cross paths with him. I high-fived him and said, "Nice one."

He said, "Thanks. Where in the UK are you from?" He had picked up on my accent.

"London," I said.

We walked around the side of the house, sat on a bench, and talked for a while. We exchanged numbers, and he told me he was staying at the Mondrian Hotel on Sunset Boulevard. He invited me to hang out later on. I had to explain that I couldn't leave the mansion—and that I had a curfew at 9:00 p.m. He laughed and said, "Let's get together tomorrow before I go back to the UK."

I slept on the idea. I woke up and decided to go see him at the hotel. I had no intention of anything sexual happening. I always assumed that guys were turned off by the fact I was Hef's girlfriend.

When I arrived, he opened the door in white Calvin Kleins, and he looked so fit and strong. I had never really been attracted to a Black man, and I had never even been with a Black man before. Still, I could feel the sexual tension between us. We were flirting. After talking for a while, he grabbed me, threw me on the bed, and climbed on top of me. I could feel him grinding on me with his extra-large penis. It made me nervous—it was so big. He started pulling my clothes off.

The moment was passionate and lustful. I couldn't resist running my hands over his hard muscles, and he smelt so good. He inserted himself, and it was enjoyably painful. As we tossed and turned, taking turns and changing positions, it was amazing. We were both sweating and hot, wet, and loud. When we had finished and recovered, I giggled to myself. I instantly felt guilty about my husband and Hef—but at the same time, I hadn't been satisfied like that in months. I didn't really know about his status in the UK, but I really liked him.

After having that experience, I realised I was missing intimacy and one-on-one interaction with someone. I felt like I needed to spend more time out of the mansion, so I joined the Equinox gym on Sunset Boulevard. I had Sheila join with me, and we went three to four times a week; it was a great place to meet new people and hot guys. It got us out of the mansion, and it was close to Lewis's school. I could pick him up after I worked out. I started spending more time with Lewis at home. The only times I left my apartment earlier than 9:00 p.m. was on Wednesdays and Fridays, our going out nights with Hef.

As time went on, our going-out group multiplied with girls. They were in town shooting for *Playboy*, or random girls we had invited out before, or girls I previously lured from the clubs. Having the extra girls was a great thing. The more girls there were, the more fun it was for Hef. I would also manipulate the girls and talk them into coming back to the bedroom with us. During the times spent in the bedroom as a group, we were all involved in unprotected sex, and I was continually contracting STDs. I was always on antibiotics, and I wanted to cut down and limit the sex participation between Hef and me. So I would lure girls home with us from the clubs and give them a speech on how it would really help their chances of becoming a Playmate if they had sex with Hef. I would guide them through it, and if I succeeded in convincing a girl to have sex with Hef, it would exempt me from having to have sex with him. This became an unspoken rule between Hef and me. I also told him I was more attracted to girls and was always happy to perform for him— whatever made him happy.

Usually Hef would finish himself off, but other times when he was extremely aroused, he would want to have anal sex. The only girl willing to do that was Holly, and that's why she was his number one. With all the girls on the bed naked and dancing around, it would be close to finishing time. We would all be keeping an eye out for Hef's next move. If he nudged Holly to lie on her tummy, we all knew what was about to happen. It was the worst, most excruciating experience every time it happened. We all knew she did not enjoy it. From the moment it started, her scream carried so much pain and humiliation. The expression on her face made me want to cry. Izabella and I would look at each other with such despair while it was happening. It was truly horrific. I have never witnessed such a disturbing situation. Those periods of two minutes remain among the worst times of my life, and they still haunt me. I couldn't even look the butlers in the face the next day. It was that disturbing, and the noise would travel all the way downstairs to the kitchens.

I started to feel a little unsettled every time we went in the bedroom, so I would get more and more intoxicated. I started doing cocaine again, and I would mix it with the quaalude that Hef gave me, drink alcohol, and smoke some weed just to get through it. I got the cocaine from one of our limo drivers; he was well connected and had a hookup for everything. Thursdays and Saturdays became hard recovery days because of how messed up I'd get the nights before. Lewis would often see me hungover on those days, too.

My birthday was coming up, along with the Mardi Gras party at the mansion. In the back of my mind, I just kept thinking, "The best birthday gift would be for my green card to come." I was looking forward to receiving my costume allowance and birthday cash so I could save it all.

My birthday dinner with Hef.

I never spent money on my outfits for our big parties at the mansion. I did work for Leg Avenue, modelling their costumes and lingerie, and I had a good relationship with the company. So I was able to have anything I wanted for free. I always got my outfits from there. None of the girls knew this at first. But being the nice person I was, I ended up telling Sheila and Izabella. One of them told Holly, who later told Hef that I wasn't using my money on outfits—just another target on my back. Holly would do anything to get me in trouble because she was so jealous of me. The only thing I could do was step up the game. In front of everyone, including Hef, I said, "If any of you girls would like to come to the Leg Avenue offices with me to get a discount on any outfits, you are more than welcome to." I deliberately said it in front of Hef so he would see that I was not being devious or secretive, and that would shut down the rumours that Holly was spreading.

Holly started making her outfits, so she would save her money too. Every time she got me in trouble for something, she would later start doing the same thing. She made her outfits to show Hef that maybe we didn't need the wardrobe allowance. She tried to get our allowances cut down in order to get rid of us all because she wanted Hef to herself.

In the end, I just let all the girls have access to Leg Avenue for costumes and outfits. That's one of the many nice things I did that backfired on me. They all took advantage of it, but as long as they were not stepping on my toes and trying to take my modelling position for the company, I didn't give a shit. I just wanted Hef to see the kind gesture and for Holly to shut up about it.

After my birthday and the party at the mansion, I looked forward to the summer, when Lewis would have summer holiday off from school. He'd get to spend more time with me and the boys next door.

CHAPTER 15

MAKING THE MOST OF MY TIME

Once the holidays were over, I started looking forward to all the awards shows we were invited to. The Grammys were coming up, and I wanted to do something totally different, something that had never been done before. I wanted to make a statement.

I thought of a great idea. I wanted to wear my velvet backless cat suit with a fedora hat, so I thought of having a Grammy painted on my back. I had my makeup artist friend Tyson Fountaine paint it. He added rhinestones and glitter, and it came out amazing. Photographs of the design appeared in *The New York Times* and some gossip magazines—my picture was everywhere! Jay Leno even made a joke about it, asking his audience if they'd seen the "Playboy Playmate who had a Grammy Award painted on her back, which is kind of ironic—she had a Grammy on her back, and later in the evening, she had a grandpa on her front!" It was hilarious. It's still on YouTube to this day!

ol would
that
[Mon-
dinner
ans
e can
) rehab.
alcohol-
tertain-
39.

ng the
his
irl-
old
le can
music in
isten to
ut two or
we
se. But
ansion
he last
becke
a British
osby."

TATTOO YOU Hugh Hefner with Zoe Gregory (r.) among his
blondterage of Playboy Playmates at Grammy Awards last night.

The tension in the house was growing. It was quite obvious now there were two sides: my team and Holly's team. Everything had become a vindictive strategy, but this was nothing new to me. It was just exhausting to put energy into the negative, and that's what kept me out of the house all day.

It had been nearly two years since I'd moved into the mansion—time was flying by, and things had changed a lot. The novelty of being at the mansion all day every day had worn off because of the bullshit with the other girls. I'd wake up, quickly go and say good morning to the animals, and be out of the house before I bumped into any of the girls or saw Hef. I'd be gone all day and get back to the gate at curfew time. The only time I saw any of the other girls was on our nights out and at the Sunday dinner and movie. This arrangement made life so much easier, even though everyone thought I was up to something. I couldn't win. Renee, Izabella, and I were the only girls who had apartments outside the mansion, so we all had somewhere to go during the day. Renee and I also had children, so Hef would know where we were spending our days. I wasn't worried about Hef.

I'd always had such a complex about my nose, and I really wanted a nose job. I went to Hef and asked if I could get one. I had to explain why I wanted it and make him understand. Hef always wanted a valid explanation before approving any surgery. He said yes. I booked my nose job with Garth Fisher. Recovery would take three weeks. I was not able to attend the nights out; it had me in the mansion, stuck in bed for a week until I felt better. I loved the results and was so happy with it. I had wanted one for years, and I trusted Garth to do good work. He had previously done Izabella's nose as well as Holly's. My nose wasn't as bad as theirs was before surgery. I had great results with mine, but some of my modelling companies thought my face had looked better before. They said I had lost a bit of a character in my face; I was so upset. Some people don't see your face the way you see it. I ended up losing a couple of recurring modelling jobs because of my new nose.

I could see Lana wasn't happy living at the mansion anymore, and I knew she was going to leave soon. I think she wanted to get back with her boyfriend. I already knew she was in her last days since she had gotten what she wanted: a new car and a new nose. She had saved a bit of money too. I think she was the one out of all of us who hated being there the most. I hooked her up with a couple of modelling jobs that I didn't want to do. We were not looking to replace her with a new girl. We were comfortable with the group as it was.

I was looking at property in the paper again. I would look for something around West Hollywood. I liked that area, but I needed to get an idea of what prices were and how much I was going to need. I had no idea about any of it, but I knew Chris did; he had bought property before, so I had him for guidance. I thought I could perhaps rent it out while I was still at the mansion and have something to move into when I decided to leave.

I contacted a real estate agent named Robert, and he took me around once a week to look at condos in the area. I told him about my situation, and he gave me a lot of advice. We contacted a broker to see if I was in a position to apply for a loan before we made any offers. My taxes were in order, but it turned out that I needed a couple more months of consistency in my bank account before I would be ready. We decided to keep looking until then. I was so happy to find out that this was all going to be possible. I was just hoping my green card would come in the next couple of months.

In April, my green card finally came. I called Chris and couldn't wait to tell Lewis. We were going to live our dream in LA, just like we'd wished and hoped for. I ran to Hef and told him too. I wanted to celebrate, and now I was comfortable with the other girls finding out because it was physically in my hand. I felt like I had won the lottery.

I called my real estate agent and told him I had my green card and was ready to find a property to buy. I found a beautiful condo in the back of the Sunday *Times* and forwarded the info to Robert. He arranged to have us go and see it the following week. Holly had frequently seen me taking the back section of the newspaper from the little green dining room downstairs. I think she knew what I was doing, but it was none of her business. I never talked to any of the girls about my next moves.

I couldn't wait till Wednesday to go out and have a drink. It hadn't sunk in yet that my green card was finally here. I still couldn't believe it. Hugh Hefner had made my dreams come true. I was going to make sure I pulled a few girls from the club as my "thank you" to him. I laugh to myself as I write this, but it's the truth.

I told the butlers about my green card. I was happy for them to leak the news, saving me from having to tell everyone. They were so happy for me. Unlike the girls—they all got jealous, but it was something that Hef didn't have to do for them. I thought they would be happy for me. I was wrong. Perhaps Holly thought now that I had my green card, I would leave the mansion. She thought that's all I wanted. She was dead wrong.

I went to meet up with the real estate agent to see the condo. It was ten minutes from the mansion. It was in West Hollywood, five minutes from Beverly Hills; the location was perfect. It was a first-floor corner unit facing the street, with a Starbucks on the corner. It had two bedrooms and an office, and it was very bright. I loved it; it was perfect. It was selling for $380,000, and Robert suggested making an offer for $365,000. We went back to his office to complete all the paperwork. I had given him my legit tax returns, my green card, and all the other documents, and I would need to write him a check for 3 percent for the deposit. I was really excited.

I didn't want to say anything to Chris or Lewis yet. I wanted to make sure it was mine first. I had no intention of having Chris move into the condo with us when that time came. Chris and I had drifted apart but remained civil. He wanted a green card too, and because we were still married at the time, he was able to apply for his through mine. He was very lucky to have acquired the visas and green card through me. All I asked him to do was pay the taxes from the previous years when I was depositing his checks. He said he would.

When someone gives me their word, I expect them to stick to it.

My real estate agent told me everything about what was involved with fees and payments when you buy property. I didn't know about any of this stuff; he guided me through everything and prepared me for what to expect if the offer was accepted. I wanted to save and save while at the mansion. I wanted to be able to decorate my place and have all the finances covered. I wasn't ready to leave the mansion just yet.

CHAPTER 16

BACKSTABBED ONCE AGAIN

I called my mum and let her know that I had received my green card and that I was about to buy a place. I felt so good about giving her this news. I was finally making her proud of me! She was ecstatic, so happy for me. She kept saying she wanted to come and visit me, but I kept putting it off. I told her I would come and see her first before she came to LA.

I asked Hef if I could go back to the UK for a couple of days to see my family. Of course he said I could, but only for a couple of days. With all that was going on, I didn't want to be gone for too long. I let my London modelling agency know that I was coming back, thinking maybe they could get me some publicity while I was there.

It turned out that *News of the World* was interested in doing a story on me living at the mansion, so my agent arranged it all and I booked my flight for the next week. I had mentioned to Izabella that I was going home to see my family, and I was maybe going to do some modelling and story work for the newspaper. She was the only one I had mentioned it to. I asked her not to say anything to anyone yet.

I flew home. I was so happy to see my mum. It had been a while, and I missed her so much. It was great to be back in the house I grew up in. The word had gotten around that I was back home, and all my old friends wanted to see me.

The next day, I went for the photo shoot to do a story for the newspaper with Jeany Savage, who was directing all photography and interviewing for the story. While I was having my makeup done, I told them some truths and exaggerated about a few things—but nothing to make Hef look bad. It was mostly about the celebrities who came to the mansion. The shoot went well, and the story was to be featured in the upcoming weekend's newspaper. I was rather excited.

I spent some time with my mum and brother. They told me that my father had a new girlfriend. I hadn't spoken to him for a while. It seemed like he was doing his own thing, and he made no attempt to contact me, so I didn't bother with trying to contact him while I was there.

I was flying back to LA the day that the newspaper was supposed to publish my story. I was at the airport when I saw a copy of it. I opened it up, and there was a double-page spread of me and the story. Unfortunately, they had edited a lot of what I said and made it seem scandalous. That was so typical of the British tabloids; they make everything sound bad.

I was concerned that if Hef saw this, he might get upset. I was a little disappointed with the editing. They had misconstrued the story. I hadn't told the story the way it was written. I called my agent and told him I might get in trouble for this. I felt like I had made a mistake. It seemed so negative; I should have known better. The British tabloids just want to write controversially and exploit you in any way possible.

EXCLUSIVE

News > World News

SICKENING PIMP SECRET
Brit model lured girls to the Playboy Mansion to have orgies with Hugh Hefner with drugs and promising them fame

When I got home to the mansion and walked into my room, the same newspaper was on my bed. Someone had put it there. The only person who would have done that was Hef. Izabella told on me; I later found out from Hef that Izabella had told Holly, and

Holly had told him. I'd been backstabbed once again. I couldn't trust any of the other girls anymore, even the ones who seemed to have my back.

Hef came to my room and sat on the floor. I knew this was going to be bad. He said I was very wrong for what I'd done. I explained to him that the tabloids had told the story a lot differently from how I'd relayed it. He of all people should have known how the media worked, but he was very upset with me. I was livid with Izabella. I couldn't believe she'd done something so nasty, and she was the only one I had told, so she couldn't lie about it being her. I didn't speak to her for a while. After all Hef had done for me, I felt terrible.

I had a lot of making up to do, but that wasn't the problem. I had never seen Hef so devastated, and that broke my heart. I truly felt awful. The mood was sombre in the house that day, and I didn't leave my room. I didn't want to talk to anyone. I would only talk to the butlers; they were my friends more so than any of the girls.

The next day, I woke up and left the house before anyone was up. I went to the gym for a few hours. While I was working out, Robert called and told me my offer for the condo had been accepted. I wanted to scream with excitement. Just when all was doomed, my day turned around. I rushed to Roberts's office, which was two minutes from the gym. I wanted to get everything done immediately! I signed all the paperwork and paid all the fees. I was one step closer to owning a home. I felt insecure about my position at the mansion, and having the condo prepared me for whatever was going to happen. That stability felt really important.

For the first time, I was dreading Wednesday night. I didn't want to see anyone. Sheila was the only person I still felt close to, as she was my friend from the start. I just had to get very drunk and under the influence to be friendly to the rest of them.

CHAPTER 17

GOING SOUTH

Even though my relationships in the house were rocky, I had everything else under control. I picked Lewis up from school and told him about the condo; we drove by it so he could see where it was. He was so happy for us. It was by his school, and his friends lived close by too. I had Lewis start staying with me at the mansion during the week, apart from Wednesdays and Fridays. He kept me company and spared me having to spend any more time with the girls. I drove him to school every morning and then went to the gym.

I was spending more and more time away from the mansion. I just felt so betrayed by the other girls. I went and looked at furniture for the condo and started shopping for bits and pieces for the new place. Sheila called to tell me that Holly went and copied me and did a story with an American magazine; she said I should go get a copy. I just couldn't believe it—even though she did the same thing, all the other girls reacted differently to her than they did to me. It was obvious most of the girls had started kissing Holly's ass. That is something I have never done and never will; I have way too much pride. I would rather leave the situation than suck up to someone I hate. It was really frustrating for me. I wanted to slap them all! I was used to physically fighting my battles, but I couldn't even confront Holly or any of the girls at this point, as I didn't want to be kicked out of the mansion just yet. I had to bite my tongue. It was one of the hardest things I had to learn to do in this situation.

I think it had been around six months since Holly and I had spoken. I'm surprised that Hef hadn't said anything, but a part of me thought that he liked the conflict of girls battling over him—even though I wasn't fighting for him, I was fighting to remain innocent in his eyes despite all the lies the girls told him.

I could feel it was the end of days for me. I knew I couldn't tolerate living there much longer, and I didn't want to get depressed at such a beautiful time of my life. I wanted this experience to be amazing, so I had to remain positive at all times. I wanted to focus on my condo and making a home with my son, and that is what I did in the coming weeks.

Around this time, there was a private party at the mansion for the X Games. The grounds were crowded with athletes and sports figures. A couple of the girls and I decided to go down and roam around the grounds. We jumped on the trampoline for a while as we observed who was there. There were quite a few familiar faces—and lots of tattoos, shaved heads, and fit bodies. It was mostly guys.

We started talking to a few guys. A couple of them were dirt-bike racers, and I found that I could relate to them since I used to joyride the same bikes when I was a kid. They also reminded me of my old friends at home. It was nostalgic. Izabella and I chatted with them both for a while, until the party ended. They invited us to the races, but we never ended up going that year.

When we went out the following Wednesday, we saw the same two guys, Ronnie and Tyler, at the club we went to with Hef and the girls. They tried to come over and talk to us, but security stopped them from approaching us past the red velvet rope. So we went to the bathroom, and on the way, we passed them to say hello.

After that, we kept seeing them at the clubs every week, and they would ask to take us out. We explained about our curfew and told them it wasn't a good time while we worked at the mansion, but they would still follow us everywhere every week. It was quite amusing. It kept us occupied at the clubs, and we'd sneak away to talk to them. Sheila thought the guys were gross. She would laugh at them; she thought they were trailer trash. It was quite funny. Our security had eyes on them; they would see them all the time hovering around us. It was becoming annoying to me that we were not allowed to talk to any other guys while we were out with Hef. I understood that it was not a good look to be seen as Hef's girls talking to other men, but I guess that's where this job started to wear on me.

I took up the habit of smoking again so I could get away from the table at the club from time to time. Sheila and I started making friends with a lot of regular people we'd see at the clubs on Wednesdays and Fridays. Most of them were local. Some were socialites, some were professionals, but they would always be there. The guys would ask us when we were moving out of the mansion so we could go out with them. Going out became fun again, now that we had a few friends we would see consistently.

I took a liking to one the guys, Jeff. He owned a tanning salon on Sunset Boulevard. He was not my usual type, but he would flirt with me all the time and tell me to come by the salon and for a free tan. So I did. I went during the week to see Jeff and to tan, even though we had tanning beds at the mansion. When I got there and asked for him at the desk, they sent me to his office down the hall. I walked in, and I instantly felt the sexual energy between us. He smelled so good—it consumed his whole office. I sat down, and we had a chat; we were both giggling and smiling and nervous. We exchanged numbers, and he said I could choose a bed to use and to come in any time. I was to call him beforehand to make sure he was there.

I knew the next time I saw him at that office, we would be all over each other. It was exciting to have this chemistry again with someone I was attracted to. I was also looking forward to seeing him at the club in the coming week; we knew we really liked each other. I couldn't wait to tell Sheila, as she was with me when Jeff and I started talking. The great thing was the tanning salon was across from my gym. It was so convenient.

Hef hadn't really shown me any attention lately, and I was constantly defending myself from gossip that Holly and Bridget would put in his head, which I suppose pushed me even more into the outside world. It felt healthy to be desired again and lusted over. I hadn't had these feelings for some time. I felt fuelled and energised. I couldn't wait to go back into the office to see Jeff.

I made a major effort on Wednesday night to dress up, which of course sparked the girls' curiosity as to why I was trying so hard. I'm sure they thought it was to butter up Hef and kiss his ass. But Sheila was the only one to know what was going on. By now I couldn't care less what the others thought.

I saw Jeff at the club. I walked over to him, and he said, "Oh my God, you are killing me right now." He told me I looked so good. I guess he liked my outfit. I knew it would drive him crazy. He said I had better go and see him in the office the next day. I couldn't wait.

The next day, I wore a skirt with no underwear and a little lace top. I went to the office and walked in. He was so excited— he reached out and put his hands on me. I was overdosing on his smell. It felt like everything was going in slow motion. He told me to come sit on him, so I straddled the office chair and sat on him. He was already hard. I could feel it through his jeans, and it felt huge—abnormally huge. He lifted up my skirt to see that I had no underwear on. That drove him crazy.

"Oh my God," he whispered. He couldn't contain himself as he started to undo his belt. I stared at his lips while biting my own, humming and heavy breathing. It was so lusty. I stood up and bent over while he pulled down his pants, and then I popped back on top of him on the chair.

I had no idea how his manhood would fit inside of me. It was the biggest I had ever seen before, but I wanted it. I began to slowly wind on him, thrusting on it while getting wet. It was hard not to be noisy. The reception was so close to his office, but that made it feel all the naughtier and more exciting. We rocked back and forth as he penetrated me deeper and deeper. His cock did not fully fit inside of me, but it was enough to feel most of him. It felt amazing. I had to have this all the time. He wanted to come, and I said, "Tell me when," so I could jump off and he could come in my mouth—and that's what we did.

It lasted the whole of seven minutes. With the buildup and the excitement, I was honestly surprised it lasted that long. We both laughed at what we had just done. He kept saying how much he loved what we just did, and how sexy I was, and how I could come by any time.

He made an account for me at the tanning salon so it would look more legitimate every time I came in. He gave me an unlimited account, and it worked perfectly. I was thrilled. I couldn't wait to tell Sheila, and I also couldn't wait to go back and see him. My body and mind really needed meaningful sex. I hadn't come that much in years.

I did soon find out that he had a girlfriend, and apparently she looked just like me. I hadn't thought I would start dating him or get into a relationship, but when I found out, it did hurt a little bit. I suppose it hurt because it had been a while since I'd felt a real emotional connection. We continued to see each other every time I went into the salon to tan, and I kept saying hi to him when we went out clubbing. I must admit we had something special. I continued seeing him for a few more years after the mansion, too.

After the encounters I had with Jeff, I started realising I needed real affection in my life before I became numb. Returning to the mansion started to sadden me. I could feel myself becoming unhappy and not willing to participate in anything. I began to plan my exit.

CHAPTER 18

FINAL MISSION

I t was a vulnerable feeling, thinking about starting a new life with my son in America, with no family, in a foreign country that I was still getting familiar with. I wanted everything to be in order. Everything had to be lined up and ready. The last thing worrying me about leaving was the tax issues with Chris. I had continued asking him to be prepared to help with paying it. It looked like it would be $5,000–$10,000. Every time I brought it up to him, he'd tell me he had no money at that moment, which really concerned me. The unresolved taxes could really interfere with everything that was going so smoothly for me. I felt betrayed by him, and I didn't believe him.

I had been at the mansion for nearly three years now, and I was so ready to leave. I remembered a Playmate saying that a very wealthy man had asked about me. I didn't quite understand where she was going with it, so I asked her to get more information. She eventually called me and proceeded to tell me that I had a big fan, a

Wall Street banker in New York who would love to have the opportunity to meet me. She told me that he had met previous Playmates and that he gave a very generous gift to meet.

I had all the information I needed, but I had to think about it. I didn't want to trust anyone. It could have been a setup, and it was too close to home. But I knew that if it got out, I had all the evidence that this Playmate had been setting up a lot of other Playmates with fans for transactions. So her secret was as valuable as mine.

The man was making a generous offer: I would go to New York and stay at the Ritz for one night, and he would come visit me during his lunch break from work. I would spend an hour with him, and he would pay me $10,000. A first-class flight and $10,000 to visit New York for a few hours sounded like a great deal. I was determined to do it, especially since it would cover me if Chris was going to let me down.

I had to make a fake work itinerary on my computer for a modelling job so I could show Hef and get permission to be released for one night. I gave the phone number of a client from a previous modelling gig. They would have my back and confirm it if anyone called. It was a bit of a risk to take, but it was worth it. I asked myself, "Is this prostitution?" But somehow, I thought what I was doing at the mansion was the same kind of thing.

My only guilt was towards my son. Morally, I felt like shit. I didn't tell anyone, not even Chris, that I was going to New York.

I checked into the Ritz-Carlton in Battery Park. The suite had the most amazing views. It was a beautiful hotel. I got a call on my cell phone saying that "Mark," the guy, would be there during his lunchtime at 1:00 p.m., so I took a shower and got ready. I closed the curtains and put on a dress.

The doorbell rang, and it was him. I let him in. He was really nice and sweet from the moment I met him, which put me at ease.

He was a little overweight, but how could I complain when I was known to be with Hef, someone who was twice my age?

Mark just wanted to talk about my life at the mansion. We continued to talk, and I was exaggerating everything. He was so excited to hear about it all. Forty-five minutes had gone by, and we had just been talking, though I knew this was only an hour visit for him.

He got up and said, "That's a pretty dress you are wearing."

Like a cliché, I said, "Oh, yes, I got it just for you."

He walked over to his jacket hanging on the back of a chair, pulled a chunky bank envelope from the inside pocket, and handed it to me. I took it and said, "Thank you so much."

He came over to me and ran his hands over my breasts. I looked at the clock by the bed, and it was 2:00 p.m. It made me feel edgy. At that point, he stepped back and said, "Can I use the bathroom?"

"Yes," I said, "of course."

When he went in, I went right to my bag and started to count the money. It all seemed to be there, including the flight money and a tip on top of that.

When he returned, he grabbed his jacket and said he'd better be heading back to work. He said it was such a pleasure to meet me, and with that, he left.

I couldn't believe I'd flown all the way to New York to meet someone, just sit and talk about the Playboy Mansion and be paid more than $10,000. All my fears had gone. I wasn't nervous anymore. I sat on the end of the bed, feeling so relieved and happy.

I got dressed and decided to go to the bank to deposit half of the money. I knew I shouldn't travel with all of it.

The next time we went out to the club, I saw Jeff from the tanning salon and told him how close I was to leaving the mansion. I said I couldn't wait to have my freedom back. He was ecstatic for me. He couldn't wait to hang out and do things together, and that made me even more excited.

I continued to prepare my condo to move in. It was close to being ready. I thought that I should soon have a sit-down with the girls—Izabella, Sheila, and Renee—and tell them that I was thinking about leaving the mansion. It felt sad to imagine.

Lewis and Cooper's band The Skips played at the Whisky a Go Go on Sunset Blvd.

It had been three years, and the first half of that time was amazing, but the last few months it had gotten really hard for me to bite my tongue. I knew that Lewis would not be happy about my decision to leave, but he would still be able to go and see the boys next door, as he had started a little music band with them, and they had band practice every weekend.

I had been speaking to my mum a lot during the previous few weeks, as I was getting close to leaving. We could finally arrange for her to come and visit. I was so excited and needed some motherly comfort. I had missed her so much. Lewis hadn't gone back to England for the past couple of years during the summer holidays. He wanted to be at the mansion with the boys, so he had missed his grandma too. With the condo being a secret, all I wanted was for someone to be proud of me, to tell me I had done a good job.

The energy at the mansion was so negative, but I really looked forward to letting them all know that despite everything, I had succeeded in saving my money, buying a property, and receiving my green card. I knew they would all be in shock when they found out. I put in work to achieve what I had, and I endured the backlash from the other girls. It had not been easy, but I made it work. I knew Hef would be proud of me when he found out that I had done something significant with the money I'd earned at the mansion.

I remember this day. I knew it was time to say something to the girls and let them know that I planned to leave in the next few weeks. When I had hinted previously, they'd said, "If you leave, I'm leaving." They claimed they didn't want to be there without me, but I never knew if they meant that.

I got back to the mansion and walked through the pantry where all the butlers were. I stopped to say hi and chat with them as I usually did. I mentioned that I wouldn't be staying much longer, and they all freaked out and wanted to know why. Well, they knew the friction that was going on in the mansion, but they assumed it was for a different reason. I told them I simply wanted to move on and be in a more positive environment, and they totally understood. I knew the news would travel around the mansion to the offices, and all the employees would hear about it in a few days. I didn't mention anything about moving into my condo yet.

I went upstairs to Sheila's room and told her first. She already knew how I was feeling, but this just confirmed my decision. She said she wanted to leave with me but didn't have anywhere to go. I thought perhaps I could rent her a room at my new condo, but I didn't say anything yet.

I went to Renee's room and told her lightly, and she said she had a feeling it was going to happen soon.

I passed by Izabella's room, popped my head in, and played a joke on her: I said, "Hef just kicked me out, so I'm coming to say goodbye." She looked at me in shock. It was a good joke, a good lead-in to what I was going to tell her. I told her I was just kidding and then continued, "But I'm thinking about leaving in the next few weeks."

She was surprised and asked why; she thought something had happened. She always wanted to investigate, but I told her it was time, and I was sick of having a bad feeling in the house. She agreed with what I was saying, and she also said she was going to leave with me. So now I would let this news marinate, and the rumour would travel through the mansion within days.

I hadn't seen Hef in a couple of days, so I went to see Norma in the office. I told her how I was feeling and that I was thinking of leaving. She was heartbroken but knew I was on my last nerve.

I didn't know how I was going to break the news to Hef. I was dreading it. I really didn't want to leave him. I was worried about what the ugly girls would put him through. How bored he would be without the cool girl gang!

The next morning, I went down to the see the animals, and my cell phone rang. It was Mary from the office. She had handed Hef the phone. He asked if I was on the mansion grounds and if I could meet him in my room. I could tell from his voice what was about to happen. I knew him so well that even from the tone of his voice, I knew. I'm so glad it happened this way, but I was still dreading it.

I went to my room. He came in five minutes later and sat on the floor with his head down. He said, "Honey, I think it's time we go our separate ways. You and Holly will cause me a heart attack if this animosity continues in the house."

I held his hand and said, "Yes, you are right." I totally agreed with him. I told him it was fine and that I understood.

He got up, and we held each other and hugged. I had a lump in my throat, and I wanted to cry. I thanked him for everything and for making my dreams come true. I felt sick to my stomach but at the same time so excited to move on. I loved Hef so much.

My hero.

EPILOGUE

I moved out of the Playboy Mansion in 2004.

Sheila moved out with me. Iz and Renee left the week after I did.

I had the most amazing experience of my life at the mansion, even with all the obstacles and challenges. I made the best decisions I could. Having acquired my green card and bought a home, I felt the good outweighed the bad in the end.

The journey of my dream come true was a rollercoaster ride. I made bad decisions, and I made some really good ones, too. Everything I did was with the best interests of my son in mind; I just wanted to provide him with a good life.

After Playboy, I am now a lot more cautious about trusting the people close to me.

I got fucked over by Brad, Chris, and the girls at the mansion—all people I trusted. But there was one person who never let me down.

Hugh Hefner was the hero of my story.

Printed in the USA
CPSIA information can be obtained
at www.ICGtesting.com
LVHW040610120124
768782LV00005B/64